WHO'S ? RIGHT

WHO'S? RIGHT

MANKIND, RELIGIONS & THE END TIMES

KELLY WARMAN-STALLINGS

authorHOUSE®

AuthorHouse™
1663 Liberty Drive
Bloomington, IN 47403
www.authorhouse.com
Phone: 1-800-839-8640

First published by AuthorHouse   01/23/2012

ISBN: 978-1-4685-3738-3 (sc)
ISBN: 978-1-4685-3739-0 (ebk)

Library of Congress Control Number: 2012901922

Printed in the United States of America

Any people depicted in stock imagery provided by Thinkstock are models, and such images are being used for illustrative purposes only.
Certain stock imagery © Thinkstock.

This book is printed on acid-free paper.

DEDICATION

To my sister, Kathy, I wish to express my thanks for the many days you spent proof-reading this book and the noteworthy input you offered.

To my brother, Kerry, for the time you took out of your own busy journalistic schedule to edit this work, I am most appreciative and honored.

To my brother, Kirk, I am grateful, as well as thankful, for the sincere devotion you put into designing the cover for this book.

Without the three of you, I would not have been able to accomplish this feat! Thank you so much and I love you all!

TABLE OF CONTENTS

While our life is pre-ordained by an immortal power,
it is the mortal that ordains their destiny.
There are two main routes destiny travels—
The road to happiness and the path to destruction.
The choices are simplistic, yet never limited.
Circumstances arrive in many forms,
sometimes disguised as coincidences, reminding the mortal
that there is a purpose under the sun for everything.
Fate, on the other hand, also produces a combination of
choice, circumstance and purpose . . .
which allows the mere mortal a rare glimpse of something
pre-ordained; an extraordinary occurrence that happens for a reason.

Destiny bestows choices; Choices bequeath circumstances;
Circumstances create purposes; Purposes produce fate;
Fate directs destiny; Destiny ordains Life.

—Kelly Waraman-Stallings

Part One: Mankind

"The Roots of Mankind"

In this modern age of increased knowledge there are two main-streamed theories concerning the origins of mankind—creation and evolution. The former is a widely assumed interpretation, which is embraced through religious faith. The latter is a comprehensive study, embraced through scientific supposition. While there are a multitude of books, internet sites and other literature dedicated to presenting logic and reason as to the origins of mankind, the following chapter is not a debate about the origins. It is rather a simplistic approach to assimilating the data related to origins.

According to the World University Encyclopedia, published in 1968, the first known man-like creature was *Pithecanthropus Erectus* (or Java Man) in the later Pliocene period when the huge mammathus (ancient elephant) roamed the earth around 500,000 B.C. During the third Glacial Age, the Heidelberg Man made his arrival on planet Earth about 100,000 B.C.

The Neanderthal Man (homo-sapien) followed around 50,000 B.C. This ancient race of people were reputed to live in Northern Europe and were attributed with inventing stone-tipped spears, bone needles and bone fish hooks. Their large, thick-boned frames were acclimated to colder temperatures. The glaciers began melting at the end of the Ice Age and it is theorized that the Neanderthal race was wiped out.

Cro-Magnon succeeded the Neanderthal about 25,000 B.C. and ruled on earth until around 10,000 B.C. when the last Ice Age made their species of people extinct. The Cro-Magnon people were acknowledged for their cave paintings and credited for the invention of the bow and arrow and weapons for hunting and fishing.

While the theory of prehistoric man is debatable, it is said to cover only a small portion of Earth's antiquated age of eras. Science proclaims that our planet is close to 4.5 billion years old! The history of mankind falls into two divisions, 1) the vast era of pre-history and 2) the historical period, which covers approximately 6,000 years.

While evolution purportedly takes form before creation, the "creation theory" is more commonly accepted because it is a recorded and documented religion-based history concerning mankind's beginnings. And, in most cases, ancient writings have been confirmed as factual events through years of theological research into antiquity. The only common bond that the "creation theory" and "evolution theory" share: so many unexplainable answers are just not forthcoming in the appeasement of mankind's curiosity.

"Creation Theory"

The "creation theory" is as old as antiquity itself and mainly based on individual opinion. According to biblical history of the ancient era, mankind was 'created and formed from the dust of the earth in God's own image' (Genesis 1:26 [KJV]). While the "creation theory" is based on belief through religious faith and consists of individual opinion, it does have a prognostic value and is basically invariable when it comes to the bigger picture.

When examined with objectivity, the "creation theory" manages to explain empirical data with as much credibility as the "evolution theory" proclaims. Many answers remain elusive and unfathomable, but mankind will never fully comprehend the "hows", which is an element of the creation/evolution controversy.

It seems like a simple theory, but it has sparked such controversy. Mankind has not been able to completely fathom the enigma of life, or the beginnings therein. This lack of understanding can sometimes create chaos for all of those who try to decipher and/or debate the "creation theory".

Among the many aspects of evolution, creationism is not accepted because no one has ever presented proper scientific proof of such a theory. In this respect, many scholars and theologians of religion believe it is presumptuous to assume a right to reject the "creation theory" because it does not explain in detail (or scientific terms) "how" the Creator performed the act of creation to begin with. Such is the act of arrogance on mankind's part. Had the Creator wanted to elaborate on the intricacies of creation and bestow such knowledge, he would have included such understanding for man to fathom out. For some scholars of science, this explanation is not "good enough", and it becomes a controversial stalemate among mankind.

The desire for knowledge is like an all-consuming fire that the waters cannot quench. Being able to discern fact from fiction becomes surreal in the search for answers. From the beginning of the historic era, answers have been elusive.

The "creation theory" is a rather simple-minded concept . . ."In the beginning God created the heavens and earth." (Genesis 1:1) With "created" being the operative word, endless generations have come to believe that this Creator made everything, including mankind.

"EVOLUTION THEORY"

According to the "evolution theory" of the modern A. D. era, mankind has evolved through a slow, gradual process from earlier forms of life per Charles Darwin's theory of natural selection. The "evolution theory" was suggested as early as the ancient era by Greek philosophers, such as Anaximander of Melitus (c/611-546 B.C.), who assumed the development of life from non-life and the evolutionary descent of man from fish.

This philosopher of antiquity, who wrote his theories in a poem [*On Nature*] is evidently credited with paving the way for such a scientific debate that would intensify into a worldwide controversy by the late 18th century (A.D.). In 1844, _Vestiges of the Natural History of Creation_ was published [anonymously] with the idea of transmutation of species. This writing gained wide public interest despite the scientific indignation and the conflicting interpretations of man's origins. However, the Quaker, Baptists and Unitarians welcomed the book's fresh, new ideas. Some believed their welcoming embrace was politically motivated in their struggle to overthrow the Church of England.

By 1859, when Charles Darwin introduced his evolutionary theory in a book called _On the Origin of Species by Means of Natural Selection_, widespread interest was once more rejuvenated. The Unitarians, as well as some liberal Anglicans, praised Darwin's thesis which created an even greater contention among the religious dominions, mainly the Christians.

After 1875, it became clear that the majority of naturalists embraced evolution. However, a sizable minority of Protestants rejected Darwin's theory because it called into question the accuracy of the Christian Bible's scriptures. By the turn of the 20th century, the greatest concern to the creationists was the issue of human ancestry. The evolutionary skeptics, creation leaders and skeptical scientists of the late 1800's were willing to adopt a figurative reading of the first chapter of Genesis (or allowed that six days of creation was not necessarily 24-hour days). According to the Christian Bible, " . . . one day to God is like a thousand years . . ." (Psalms 90:4 [KJV]). But, that is as far as the compromise was met on the "evolution theory."

Theodosius Dobzhansky published _Genetics and the Origins of Species_ in 1937. This book, which combined Mendelian genetics with Darwinian natural selection, explained that neutral mutation (the source of the variation upon which evolution acts) led to a combination that brought together different fields of biology and other sources into a logical explanation of evolution. Not long after Dobzhansky's publication, a crusade ensued to urge schools to teach the "fact" of evolution.

In the 1960's, the Biological Sciences Curriculum's Study (BSCS) textbooks were introduced into the nation's school systems. It was not long afterward that anti-evolutionary forces stepped in and successfully condensed the number of school districts using the BSCS biology textbooks. It is interesting to note that while the biology books were encased in a prohibition, the court system of our country continued to prevent religious instruction in public schools. (Engel v. Vitale, 1962; Murray v. Curlette, 1963)

The "creation verses evolution controversy" continues to this day with the scientific consensus on the origins of life being actively criticised by creationist organizations and religious groups who uphold the theory of creation and stands fast on their views.

While the "evolution theory" suffers from stark drawbacks, it is not much different than other philosophical or religious opinions about the origins of mankind. It is supported by some facts and refuted by others.

"Comparison of the Origins of Theories"

The following chart covers a few empirical comparisons in the creation/evolution controversial debate, published by Timothy Wallace in his literary work, _A Theory of Creation, A Response to the Pretense that No Creation Theory Exists_ (2000).

Comparison of the Evolutionary & Creationary Origins Theories

Phenomenon/Condition	Creation Hypothesis	Evolution Hypothesis
Predominant _a priori_ Assumptions (ie: Philosophical Basis) concerning the Nature, Source, and Limits of Knowledge	As with all man's endeavors, true science will inevitably honor the Creator and affirm the Bible as His true and accurate record, wherever it addresses the historical past	Man's scientific endeavors will inevitably affirm man's autonomy and independence in determining what is true and what is false
Empirically Falsifiable?	No	No
Empirically Falsified?	No	No
Predominant approach to the Bible	The biblical record is accepted as a reliable historical basis of interpreting empirical data	The biblical record is rejected as a reliable historical basis, and replaced with strict philosophical naturalism as a basis of interpreting empirical data
Empirically Falsifiable?	No	No
Empirically Falsified?	No	No
The Ice Age	Post-Flood climate compensation	Unknown
Empirically Falsifiable?	No	No
Empirically Falsified?	No	No
Massive amounts of Coded Genetic Information	Inherent and complete in original populations as created; sum total has steadily declined over time via mutational degradation	Increased over time from zero via DNA copying errors (i.e., mutations), natural selection, and millions of years
Empirically Falsifiable?	Yes	Yes
Empirically Falsified?	No	Yes

The thoroughly-researched theories of "creation/evolution" continue to be a stalemate among mankind in our modern times. While the world is billions of years old and the universe is infinitely timeless, mankind is like a newborn babe still being nursed by its mother in comparison.

power and ruled 61 years in Egypt. He was known as the "King of Persecution". He built cities, magnificent temples, the Great Wall (30 miles long) and introduced polygamy in Egypt (c/1373).

▸▸ Siculi, from Italy, settled Sicily (c/1293); the beginning of the Twentieth Dynasty of Thebes (1280) came into power.

▸▸ Assyria and Babylon united under Tiglathninip I. He was the first to assume the title, "King of Nations" as the king of Sumir and Akkad (1271).

▸▸ Hercules became ruler in Myenae (1240); Rimmon became king of Babylon, beginning its separation from Assyria (1230).

▸▸ Philistine and Ammonite oppression of Israel began and lasted 18 years; the decline of Egypt began and much art work and literature were lost to antiquity.

▸▸ The Greeks, under the command of Agamemnon, besieged the city of Troy for 10 years and eventually destroyed that ancient city. (Trojan Horse enters history about 1184 B.C.)

▸▸ The Theocracy of the Israelites ended and the Jewish Monarchy began. Saul (son of Kish, from the tribe of Benjamin), became the first king of Israel (1095).

▸▸ The Hebrew kings, David and Solomon, became strong as the Assyrians became weak; David (son of Jesse, from the tribe of Judah) became king of Israel in 1055 B.C. and Solomon (son of David) became king in 1015 B.C. (Both kings carried on the godly birthright of Seth, son of Adam)

1000-500 B.C.:

▸▸ Solomon died and the fight for his kingdom ensued, resulting in the Great Schism that caused the twelve tribes of Israel to divide. The tribes of Benjamin and Judah maintained Jerusalem as their capitol, which became the Kingdom of Judah under the rule of Rehoboam, who reigned 17 years. The kingdom continued, with 20 kings from the reign of Solomon.

▸▸ The other 10 tribes of Israel revolted and became the Kingdom of Israel under the rule of Jeroboam, who reigned 21 years. The kingdom continued, with 19 kings from the reign of Solomon and Israel's capitol became Samaria (957).

▸▸ Dayan II became king of Assyria (930); Benhadad became king of Syria (925); Nebo-Baladan became king of Babylon and a boundary was predetermined by a treaty with Assyria (880).

▸▸ Romulus, founder of Rome, was born in 770 and his kingdom was established in 753; Tiglathpileser II became king of Assyria and conquered Babylon (745); the two kingdoms united as one under the rule of Shalmaneser IV.

- The Kingdom of Israel came to an end. Samaria was overthrown and the ten northern tribes of Israel were carried away into Assyria, never to return to their sacred land. These ten tribes are referred to as the "Lost Tribes of Israel".

- Babylon was destroyed and Jerusalem was besieged by Assyria (700); Manasseh became king of Judah and ruled 55 years; Esarhaddon restored Babylon (651); Amon became king of Judah (643).

- Rome flourished under the rule of Tarquin (616); Babylon was invaded and the prophet Daniel was taken away into bondage (606); Nebuchadnezzar became king of Babylon and ruled 43 years.

- Babylon invaded Jerusalem and brought Jewish independence to an end (588); from this time on, the Jews were under the rule of Babylon, Persia, Egypt, Syria and Rome until 70, when they were scattered around the world.

- Confucius was born in China (559); Cyrus conquered Babylon; Darius became ruler (538); Zerubbabel, governor of Jerusalem, was sent to Judah to rebuild the temple (536).

- The dynasty of the Pharaohs ended and Egypt became a Persian Province (527); Confucius remodeled the sacred books of the Chinese (520); the ruler of Carthage made the first alliance with Rome (503).

500-1 B.C.:

- Herodotus, considered the "father of history", was born (484); Euripides, the Greek playwright, was born (480); Socrates, the Greek philosopher, was born (469); Hypocrites, referred to as the "Father of medicine", was born (460); Plato, the Greek philosopher and mathematician, was born (429).

- Artaxerxes II Mnemon became the king of Persia (405); Delhi was founded in India (400); the 24 books of the Jewish Tanakh (Old Testament of Christian Bible) were completed; 400 years of biblical silence started (397); Aristotle, the Greek philosopher, was born (384); Philip II became king of Macedon and first married Olympias, then Cleopatra (359).

- Alexander the Great became king of Macedon at the age of 20 years and swept across the then known world, creating the Macedonian (Greek) Empire and bringing the Persian Empire to an end. Alexander the Great died at the age of 33 years and his kingdom was divided into eight regions (323); Rome raged war and made conquests everywhere.

- The sundial of L. Papirius divided the ancient time into hours (293) ; the Alexandrian Library was built by Plolemy-Philadelpohus and contained 700,000 volumes (284); the Parthian kingdom was started; Arsaces was the first ruler (250).

- ‣ The Great Wall of China, which extended 1,500 miles was completed (236); Hannibal, who came into Carthage power in 220 B.C., defeated the Romans (221).

- ‣ The Jewish Sanhedrin was first mentioned (198); the Septuagint (Greek Bible) was translated and transcribed at Alexandria, in Egypt, by 70 Hebrew scholars at the authorization of the Sanhedrin in Jerusalem (195).

- ‣ Macedon was conquered by Rome (168); the Jews signed a treaty with the Romans (this is the first treaty with the Jews on record) (161); Greece became a Roman province under the name of Athens and finally brought the Greek Empire to an end.

- ‣ Cicero, Roman orator and philosopher, was born in this era; the Government of the Maccabees began in Palestine with Janneus as king of the Jews (106); Britain was first known as an island, having first been discovered by the Romans, who sailed around it (84); Alexandra, widow of Janneus, became queen of the Jews (79); Hyrcanus became ruler of the Jews (69).

- ‣ First Triumvirate of Julius Caesar, Crassus and Pompey were formed (60); the Parthian kingdom was destroyed by Crassus (53); the Sanhedrin took over as ruler of the Jews; Syria became a part of Rome (48); Julius Caesar, Roman dictator for four years, was slain in the Senate House by Brutus and Cassius (44).

- ‣ Egypt became a province of Rome (30); Augustus Caesar became the first Emperor of Rome (27); the Apostle Peter was born (10); John the Baptist was born (c/05).

- ‣ Jesus of Nazareth (from the lineage and godly birthright of Seth) was born (c/04) ; the ancient era of B.C. (Before Christ) comes to an end after 4,000 years and the modern era, A.D. (*Anno Domini*), begins.

1-500 A.D.:

- ‣ The Apostle Paul was born (05); Tiberius Caesar became emperor of Rome and his tyrannical reign lasted 22 years (14); John the Baptist was beheaded (c/27); Jesus was crucified (c/28); Agrippa became king of the Jews, Caligula became emperor of Rome and Flavius Josephus, the Jewish historian, was born (37).

- ‣ The first council of the Apostles was held at Jerusalem (50); the tyrant emperor, Nero, came to power in Rome (54); the Apostle Paul was martyred (68).

- ‣ Titus, the Roman emperor, captured Jerusalem with an army of 60,000 in the year 70 (1,100,000 men perished in the most horrific battle mankind had suffered since the beginning of the world.) This was the first Jewish-Roman war.

- ‣ The Apostle John was banished to the Island of Patmos (95); the 27 books of the New Testament (Christian Bible) were completed (96); Adrian became emperor of Rome and rebuilt Jerusalem (117); Christian apostles successfully spread ministries throughout

Britain (178); Lucius, the first Christian king, ruled in Britain and founded the Archbishop of York (179).

▸▸ Constantine the Great became the first Christian emperor of Rome and made Constantinople the capitol of the Roman Empire (306); the first Ecumenical Council, at which the "Nicene Creed" was adopted, was held (325); the terrible invasion of the Huns occurred (374).

▸▸ Theodosius I, ruler of Rome, officially divided the great empire of Rome into the Greek (Eastern) Empire, with the capitol being retained at Constantinople; the Roman (Western) Empire had capitols at Milan and Ravenna (395).

▸▸ Belgium revolted from Rome and set Germany in motion for gaining their independence (409); St. Patrick, a Christian missionary, arrived in Ireland (432); the empire of the Huns, under the leadership of Attila and Bleda, ravaged Europe (433).

▸▸ The fall of the Western Roman Empire occurred in 476 under the rule of Romulus Augustulus, which officially brought an end to the Roman Empire; the Eastern Greek Empire fell in 480; the "Middle Ages" started and the rise of the feudal system began.

500-1000 A.D.:

▸▸ Mohammed, the Islamic prophet, was born (c/569); St. Augustine, a Christian philosopher and theologian, arrived in England and brought with him 40 monks (596).

▸▸ Mohammed began preaching and the Qur'an was written (610); Muslim Spain emerged under the rule of the Emirs (714); Papal Rome began (755).

▸▸ Tai Tsong became emperor of China and the first government of Russia was established (762); Europe began to take shape (as we know it today) during this era.

1000-1500 A.D.:

▸▸ Muslim Spain was divided into independent states (1031); William the Conqueror [the first Norman king of England] became ruler of Normandy (1035); the Crusades began. There were eight crusades that occurred from 1096 to 1099 and it was considered one of the worse times in Christian history; Crusaders captured Jerusalem and gave the Christians control of the holy city (1099).

▸▸ The city of Moscow was built (1157); Genghis Khan founded the Mongul monarchy (c/1164); the Monguls, under the leadership of Kublai Khan, overtook China (1260).

▸▸ A papal vacancy took place for two years (1269); John Wickliffe, the English philosopher and theologian, was born in Yorkshire, England (c/1323) and the Wickliffe Bible was translated (1380).

- The "Czars" of Russia ruled from 1482 to 1698; Martin Luther, a German theologian and founder of the Reformation movement, was born (1483); the American continent was officially discovered by Christopher Columbus (1492).

1500-2000:

- Nostradamus, the prophetic seer of Jewish descent, was born (1503); Martin Luther broke away from the Roman Catholic Church (1517) and Protestantism was incorporated by him as a new religion (1529); Robert Stephens, an English scholar, sectioned the Christian Bible into verses (1551).

- Fierce religious wars spread throughout Europe as the new religious faiths were born and religious turmoil set in (1563); Galileo, the great astronomer, was born (1564); Bishop's Bible was created (1568); the Dutch discovered Australia (1606); Jamestown, Virginia became the first settlement in the American "New World" (1607); the authorized King James Version of the Christian Bible was published (1611); Wickliffe's New Testament was printed (1731).

- The United States of America was founded and George Washington was instated as its first president (1776); the American Revolutionary War commenced until the British were defeated (1783).

- Napoleon Bonaparte came to power and took the Pope prisoner (1798); Napoleon became emperor of France (1804); Napoleon was banished from England after the Battle of Waterloo (1815). The Napoleonic War claimed over 3,000,000 lives, making this now the second worst battle in history to date.

- Joseph Smith, an American religious leader, introduced the Book of Mormon (1817) and the Mormon Church was founded in upstate New York (1830); Protestants experienced the "Great Disappointment" when the "second coming of Jesus Christ" did not occur (1844).

- The Italian army took Rome (1870); the Wright Brothers flew the first manned flight (1903); after the assassination of Archduke Franz Ferdinand of Austria, Germany led the planet into World War I (1914).

- The British captured Jerusalem and Islamic rule in Palestine ended as the Turkish-Ottoman Empire was destroyed in 1923 (this battle for power began in 1299). Jews were allowed to return to the Holy Land, ending an 1,800 year lockout.

- Communism seized power in Russia and set up an anti-religion state; America officially declared war on Germany, entering World War I (1917).

- Benito Mussolini, the 40th Prime Minister of Italy, signed a treaty that officially separated church and state and subjected the Roman Catholic Church to a small area of sovereignty in Rome; Vatican City was formed, an action that fundamentally canceled the final remnants of the Theodosus decree (1929).

▸▸ The Great Depression swept across the world (1929); Adolph Hitler, a German dictator and considered the world's worst persecutor, led Germany and the world into World War II and the Jewish Holocaust began (1939). For the third time in history, this becomes the worst war of mankind, with Hitler executing over 6,000,000 people; 3,000,000 Jews lost their lives during this war.

▸▸ The atomic bomb was invented and dropped on two Japanese cities (Hiroshima & Nagasaki) by America and World War II came to an end (1945); the Cold War began and the United Nations were formed (1947); the Jewish nation of Israel was founded by a United Nations' mandate (1948).

▸▸ Communists launch war in Korea (1950); the hydrogen bomb was invented (1953); America entered the Vietnam War (1964); Israel defeats the Arab rule of the Holy Land in the Six Day War and reclaimed Jerusalem as their nation's capital (1967).

▸▸ The United States landed on the moon (1969); the AIDS plague publicly began (1981); the First Persian Gulf War broke out (1990).

▸▸ Communism crumbled and the Soviet Union was dissolved; the first Gulf War ended (1991); Eastern Europe ended the Cold War (1992); the world's population increased to six billion people (1999).

▸▸ Terrorists attacked America and the Afghanistan War began; (2001) the Iraq War, also known as the Second Persian Gulf War, began (2003).

▸▸ Barack Hussein Obama, a descendant of Muslim bloodlines, becomes president of the United States of America (2009).

▸▸ The world's population increased to seven billion people (2011).

▸▸ Natural disasters in the 21st century are becoming more common and frequent on Planet Earth: India [8.1] Earthquake (2001); Iran [6.6] Earthquake (2003); Indonesian Tsunami [underwater earthquake 9.0] (2004); United States Hurricane [C5] Katrina (2005); Myanmar [C5] Cyclone (2008); China [7.5] Earthquake (2008); Haiti [7.0] Earthquake (2010); Chili [8.8] Earthquake (2010); Sumatra [7.5] Earthquake (2010); Japan [9.0] Earthquake and Tsunami (2011); Iceland Volcanic Eruption (2011); Deadly American [T5] Tornadoes (2011); Japan [7.5] Earthquake (2011); Chili Volcanic Eruption (2011); New Zealand [7.8] Earthquake (2011); Multitude of October 23rd Earthquakes [5.1; 5.6; 6.0; 4.9; 7.2] hit Turkey (2011); Massive Bangkok Flooding (2011).

The total estimated death toll of these major disasters was well over 1,000,000 lives. In the first decade of the 21st century, the increase in natural disasters upon our planet was quite alarming.

Not only have major earthquakes struck, cyclones torn through villages and hurricanes deluged many coastal lines, but sleeping giants such as volcanoes, unexpected typhoons and blizzards without warnings have descended upon planet Earth.

Between 2000 and 2010, there were 46 major earthquakes; 33 recorded landslides/mudslides; 25 reported avalanches; 17 active volcanoes; 12 major hurricanes; 10 major typhoons; 5 major tsunamis; and 3 major cyclones.

These figures do not include the many tornadoes, floods, forest fires, heat waves and blizzards that has came upon the world in the last ten years. Scientists proclaim that the natural course of the Earth is apparently waking up and for mankind to take notice and prepare for what is to come.

"Genealogical Timeline"

According to Christian, Islamic and Jewish ancient history, the world's civilizations were descended from a common set of parents known as Adam and Eve.

The Holy Bibles of the world state that Adam was created from the dust of the Earth and life was given to him when the Creator blew life into his nostrils. Eve was created in the same manner, with the exception of receiving one of Adam's ribs. The Creator planted a garden [Garden of Eden] and instructed man to "work it and watch over it" (Gen. 2: 15 [KJV]).

The first man and woman was allowed to eat from any tree in the garden except for the Tree of Knowledge of Good and Evil, "for on the day you eat of it you shall surely die" (Gen. 2: 17 [KJV]). The historical man and woman disobeyed their Creator and did eat from the Tree of Knowledge.

Soon after, they were evicted from their fruitful garden and faced many hardships for the remainder of their lives. Other sources of theological research insist that Adam had a wife named Lilith before the creation of Eve.

Her detailed story dates back to the 13th century (AD) and can be found in the Zohar (Book of Splendor) and the Alphabet of Ben Sira (religious texts that surfaced during Medieval times and based upon traditions dating back to antiquity).

Lilith, who was briefly referenced in the Christian Bible/Jewish Tanakh (Isaiah 34:14) and who scarcely appears in the Jewish Talmud, was a prominent literary figure of Mesopotamian mythology as well.

Modern biblical scholars attribute the creation of Lilith to the first mention of woman in Genesis 1:27 [KJV]; Eve is conceived as the second mention of woman in Genesis 2:22 [KJV].

There are many legends attributed to this figure named Lilith, but all agree she was a female demon and a bearer of disease, illness, and death.

While it is a debatable subject among mankind today, Lilith was purported to bare demon offspring to Adam, as well as his firstborn son, Cain.

Some theologians believe that Lilith was made at the same time as Adam, attached to his hip, and God separated them.

Other sources contend that Lilith was born out the Great Abyss (Underworld).

Regardless of her beginnings, she was evicted from the Garden of Eden and Eve was created. This time the female would become subservient to the man and God took one of Adam's ribs and gave to Eve as a covenant for female submission.

The following charts enumerate the pre-flood descendants of Adam, the post-flood descendants of Noah and the ancient descendants of Abraham. The "godly birthright" lineages descended from Adam to Jesus Christ are in bold print.

Speculation grows as to the contrary lineages of Jesus Christ in the New Testament of the Christian Bible (Matthew 1:1-16; Luke 3:23-38), but theologians believe that Matthew is an account Joseph's lineage and Luke is a testament of Mary's lineage.

In the ancient era, the Israelite nation was enumerated according to the male head of the family.

If a Hebrew wife had a deceased father, her husband would become head of that family; although, no proof exists that Joseph was enumerated as the head of family for Mary's father's house.

The Pre-Flood Descendants:

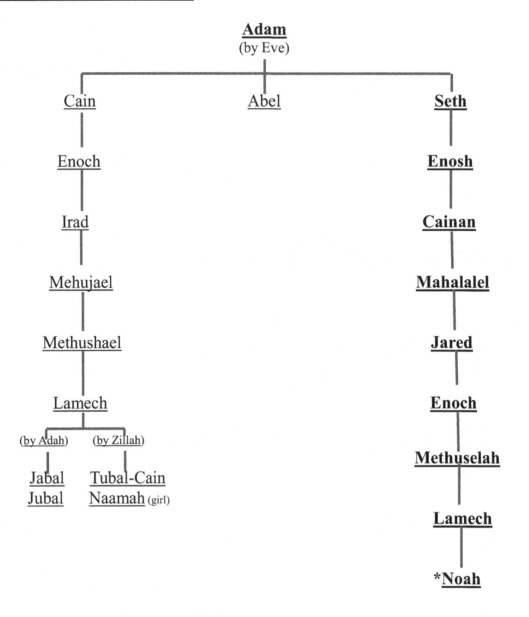

These are the heads of households and pre-flood descendants of Adam. According to the Christian Bible, the forefathers of Seth's lineage were able to lead a long and fulfilling life and died prior to the Great Flood. Cain's lineage was not as fortunate as their lives were spent in oppressive hardship.

Methuselah (who lived to be 969 years old) was the grandfather of Noah and his name meant . . . 'At his death, it will come'. Methuselah died the year of the Great Flood.

*Noah's lineage continues on the next page.

The Post-Flood Descendants:

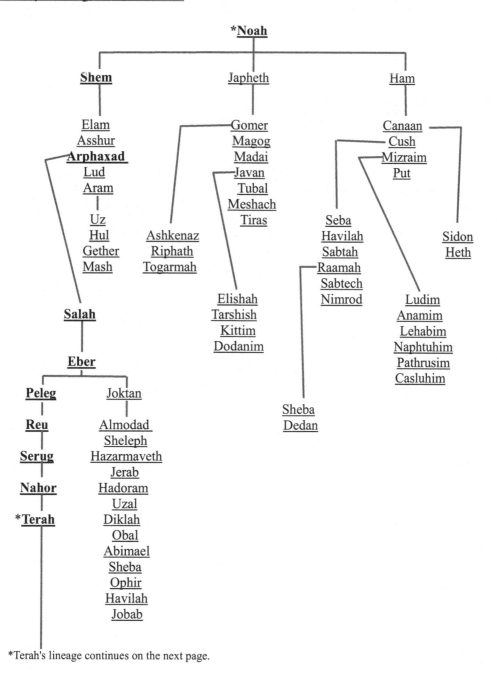

*Terah's lineage continues on the next page.

These are the generations of Noah after the Great Flood. There are ten generations from Noah to Terah (father of Abraham).

It is interesting to note that the repopulating of the ancient world was done through three lineages and, coincidentally, there are three major religions today (Christianity, Islam and Judaism). The majority of other religions teach certain aspects from one or more of the major religions

The Ancient Descendants:

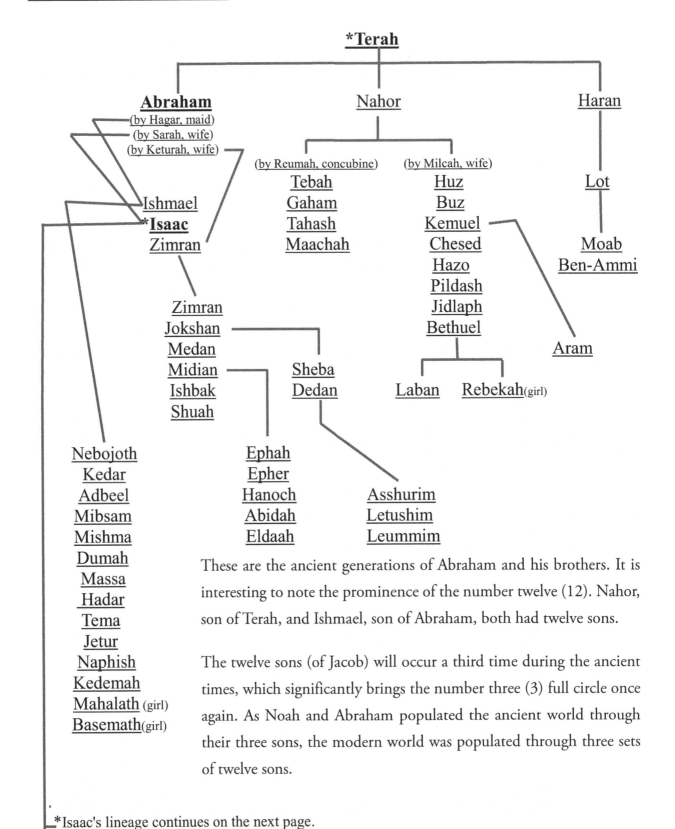

These are the ancient generations of Abraham and his brothers. It is interesting to note the prominence of the number twelve (12). Nahor, son of Terah, and Ishmael, son of Abraham, both had twelve sons.

The twelve sons (of Jacob) will occur a third time during the ancient times, which significantly brings the number three (3) full circle once again. As Noah and Abraham populated the ancient world through their three sons, the modern world was populated through three sets of twelve sons.

*Isaac's lineage continues on the next page.

The Ancient Descendants Continued:

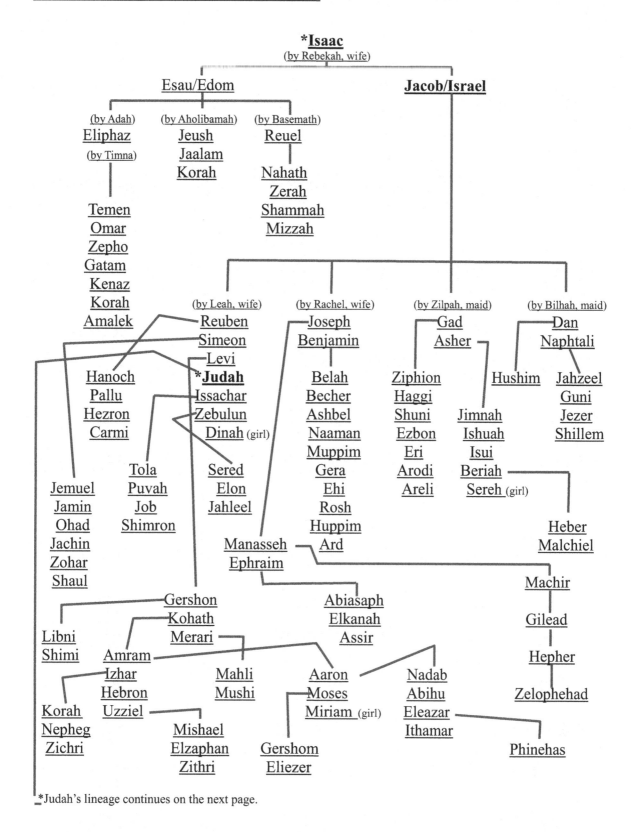

*Isaac
(by Rebekah, wife)

Esau/Edom   **Jacob/Israel**

(by Adah)   (by Aholibamah)   (by Basemath)
Eliphaz   Jeush   Reuel
(by Timna)   Jaalam
                   Korah   Nahath
                                        Zerah
                                        Shammah
Temen   Mizzah
Omar
Zepho
Gatam
Kenaz
Korah   (by Leah, wife)   (by Rachel, wife)   (by Zilpah, maid)   (by Bilhah, maid)
Amalek   Reuben   Joseph   Gad   Dan
                   Simeon   Benjamin   Asher   Naphtali
                   Levi
Hanoch   *Judah   Belah   Ziphion   Hushim   Jahzeel
Pallu   Issachar   Becher   Haggi   Guni
Hezron   Zebulun   Ashbel   Shuni   Jimnah   Jezer
Carmi   Dinah (girl)   Naaman   Ezbon   Ishuah   Shillem
                                        Muppim   Eri   Isui
                   Tola   Gera   Arodi   Beriah
                   Puvah   Sered   Ehi   Areli   Sereh (girl)
Jemuel   Job   Elon   Rosh
Jamin   Shimron   Jahleel   Huppim
Ohad   Heber
Jachin   Manasseh   Ard   Malchiel
Zohar   Ephraim
Shaul   Machir

                   Gershon   Abiasaph
                   Kohath   Elkanah   Gilead
                   Merari   Assir
Libni
Shimi   Amram   Mahli   Aaron   Nadab   Hepher
                   Izhar   Mushi   Moses   Abihu
                   Hebron   Miriam (girl) Eleazar   Zelophehad
Korah   Uzziel   Ithamar
Nepheg   Mishael
Zichri   Elzaphan   Gershom   Phinehas
                             Zithri   Eliezer

*Judah's lineage continues on the next page.

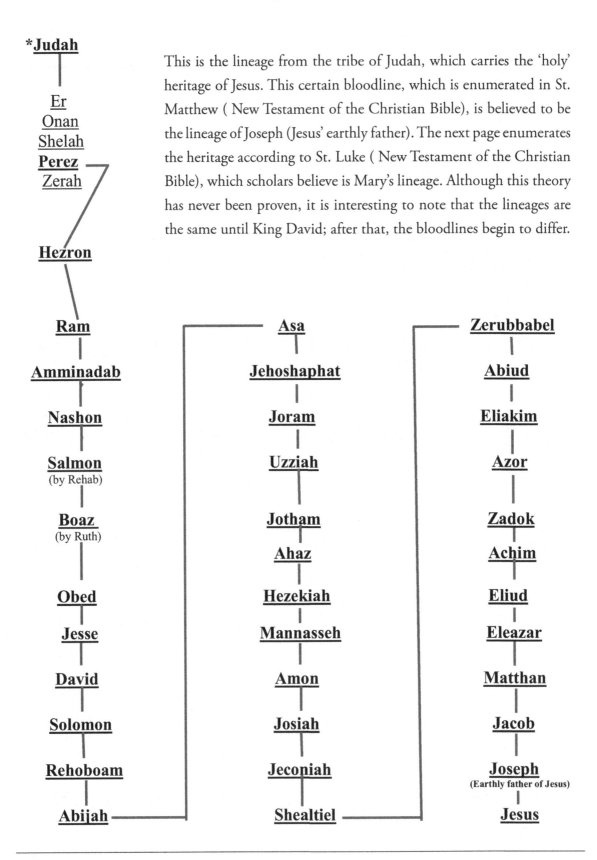

*Judah

Er
Onan
Shelah
Perez
Zerah

Hezron

Ram

Amminadab

Nashon

Salmon
(by Rehab)

Boaz
(by Ruth)

Obed

Jesse

David

Solomon

Rehoboam

Abijah

Asa

Jehoshaphat

Joram

Uzziah

Jotham

Ahaz

Hezekiah

Mannasseh

Amon

Josiah

Jeconiah

Shealtiel

Zerubbabel

Abiud

Eliakim

Azor

Zadok

Achim

Eliud

Eleazar

Matthan

Jacob

Joseph
(Earthly father of Jesus)

Jesus

This is the lineage from the tribe of Judah, which carries the 'holy' heritage of Jesus. This certain bloodline, which is enumerated in St. Matthew (New Testament of the Christian Bible), is believed to be the lineage of Joseph (Jesus' earthly father). The next page enumerates the heritage according to St. Luke (New Testament of the Christian Bible), which scholars believe is Mary's lineage. Although this theory has never been proven, it is interesting to note that the lineages are the same until King David; after that, the bloodlines begin to differ.

The Ancient Descendants according to Luke 3:23-38:

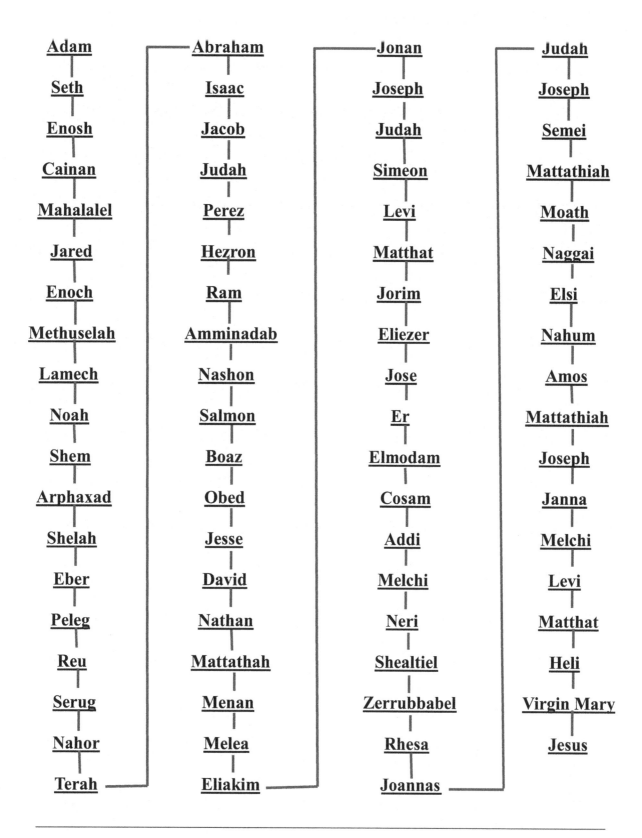

Adam — Seth — Enosh — Cainan — Mahalalel — Jared — Enoch — Methuselah — Lamech — Noah — Shem — Arphaxad — Shelah — Eber — Peleg — Reu — Serug — Nahor — Terah

Abraham — Isaac — Jacob — Judah — Perez — Hezron — Ram — Amminadab — Nashon — Salmon — Boaz — Obed — Jesse — David — Nathan — Mattathah — Menan — Melea — Eliakim

Jonan — Joseph — Judah — Simeon — Levi — Matthat — Jorim — Eliezer — Jose — Er — Elmodam — Cosam — Addi — Melchi — Neri — Shealtiel — Zerrubbabel — Rhesa — Joannas

Judah — Joseph — Semei — Mattathiah — Moath — Naggai — Elsi — Nahum — Amos — Mattathiah — Joseph — Janna — Melchi — Levi — Matthat — Heli — Virgin Mary — Jesus

While the scientific community believes the universe began 15 billion years ago, according to the Big Bang Theory, the scientists have not been able to fully comprehend or explain where the human race truly came from. It proceeds to be a stalemate project as they dig deeper in their research for the complex beginnings of mankind.

While the minority ideal of prehistoric man once existing on this planet is not a subject agreed upon by all, the written history of mankind—accepted by the majority of people—stands fast as a testimonial of whom we [humankind] are and where we came from.

Human beginnings have been a controversial topic for the last two hundred years, if not longer, and the author does not foresee that the controversy will be dissolved. Rather, this subject has escalated in mankind's search for answers. Whether one believes that mankind was created or evolved, it will remain a subject of individual belief, thought, and opinion. The knowledge of where the human race originally came from continues to remain the greatest mystery of mankind.

Part Two: Religions

"Religions of the World"

It has been estimated that there are over 30,000 different religions in the world today. With such an incredibly extensive figure, it would literally take many decades, if not centuries, to thoroughly research such vast information!

The mere problem in defining what "religion" means has produced a large ordination of scholarly works that are oftentimes in conflict and debate with one another. Some believe religion is merely a man-made vocation, brought about by the politics of mankind; while others think religion is a necessary means of connecting with a higher power.

However, the essence of religion can be understood only by following the history of various religions of mankind and comparing them. In doing so, one may find the common denominator of them all.

The difference between religion and theology is that religion is something subjective (personal) and limited through the thoughts of the individual about one or many supreme beings. Theology, on the other hand, represents an objective (impersonal) system in which beliefs and ideas are defined.

This chapter covers the basic elements of commonly recognized religions, with an emphasis being put upon Christianity, Islam and Judaism. The common element contained within any religion is based upon the belief in one god, many gods or no god at all. Such elements fall into the following categories:

1) Monotheism—belief in one god.

2) Polytheism—belief in many gods.

3) Henotheism—belief in one god superior to all others.

4) Deism—belief in one god, but believes in the rejection of God's supernatural powers and being indifferent to mankind.

5) Atheism—belief there is no god or gods.

It has been suggested by many scholars and theologians, that all forms of religion are historically connected and related to each other; however, this aspect has not been appropriately proven. In this respect, the popular meaning of the word "religion" would be better defined as a "religious creed."

"CHRISTIANITY"

While Christianity actually started with Jesus Christ and his disciples, it was not recognized until after Jesus' crucifixion in c/28 of the 1st century (A.D.). In the year 65, an organization was founded at Antioch, in Syria, which assumed the name "Christians"; soon the doctrine of Christianity spread throughout the Roman Empire by traveling apostles.

Before the end of the 1st century, Christian societies were founded in Palestine, Asia Minor, Syria, Greece, Italy, northern Africa and the islands of the Mediterranean Sea. By the beginning of the 4th century, one-third of the inhabitants of the Roman Empire had embraced the Christian religion, which was credited to the edicts of Constantine the Great. Those same proclamations made Christianity a state religion by the year 326. These early Christians were responsible for paving the way for a "religious creed" that has last for nearly 2,000 years.

Christianity is divided into three main branches: Roman Catholic, Greek Orthodox and Protestant. The Roman Catholic and Greek Orthodox, by far, are the oldest Christian sects and was once united as a singular creed. It was during the Medieval Era (2nd to 8th century) that divisions appeared in the form of political opposition and the two churches separated. The separation became definite in the 11th century.

The Roman Catholic Church declares that on the basis of Christ's original teachings, the authoritative doctrines are guided by the Spirit of God. The teachings are based on scriptures and tradition, which is set forth distinctly in the Apostle's Creed, Nicene Creed and Athanasian Creed. There are seven sacraments recognized: baptism, confirmation, the Eucharist, penance, holy orders, matrimony and extreme unction. In 1564, Pope Pius IV added the articles on the invocation of Saints. The dogma of the immaculate conception of the Holy Mother Mary was added in 1854. And, in 1870, the papal infallibility was recognized and accepted. The Roman Catholic Church also added the belief in Purgatory and the necessity of confession.

The doctrinal creeds of the Greek Orthodox Church, even today, are essentially those of the Roman Catholic Church. However, the authority of the Greek Orthodox Church does not reside in one person or structure, but the limits of jurisdiction have followed the national lines. Hence the political difference that divided the Roman and Greek Churches and brought about what was known as the Great Schism of 1054. There is no recognizable unity among the national groups and the Greek Orthodox Church, other than the fact that they do not acknowledge the authority of the Pope. The only other difference between the Roman and Greek Churches is that Greek Orthodox allows the priest to marry and have families, but only if he is unwed before he accepts the priesthood. Over the years, several attempts were made to reunite the Roman Catholic and Greek Orthodox, notably at the Council of Florence (in 1498), but none have fully succeeded in bringing them back together, even unto this day.

The Protestants include Christian denominations which are not Roman Catholic or Greek Orthodox. The Protestant Movement was started by Martin Luther, a German priest, in the early 16th century when controversy arose in the form of Luther's published _95 Thesis_ (in 1517) which theologically laid importance on faith in salvation by grace.

Luther believed every Christian was directly responsible to God and did not need the mediation of a priest (the Islamic and Jewish faith believes this as well). This belief thusly broke down the distinction between the religious and the secular, which brought about what was known as the Reformation.

Among the fundamental doctrines of Protestantism are: supremacy of the Holy Bible above bishops and councils, individual responsibility and justification by faith, prayer, and worship. The Protestants, like the Greek Orthodox, deny the authority of the Pope and hold to the right of private judgment in the matter of religion.

The universalism of Western civilization was inexplicably destroyed, causing the Christian world to disassemble. Today, many branches of the Protestant Church are widely distributed throughout the world. Among the major Protestant denominations are the Lutherans, Presbyterians, Reformed, Anglicans, Baptists, and Methodists. There are many smaller Protestant sects that branched off the major denominations, such as Evangelicals, Unitarians, Episcopalians and more.

While Christianity is divided into many religious creeds and sects, nearly all Christian bodies agree, with respect to certain cardinal doctrines, and are united in the acceptance that Jesus Christ is the Revealer of God and the Savior of mankind. Today, the majority of Christians are found in Australia, Europe, and North America, with smaller sects spread out worldwide.

"ISLAM"

This form of religion was introduced by the Prophet Mohammed ibn 'Abd Allah in 610 A.D. After announcing to his family that the angel Gabriel had given a revelation to him, Mohammed began preaching the words he received. Not long after this, the religious creed of Islam (also known as Mohammedanism) was distinguished from Buddhism, Christianity and Judaism.

In 622, his followers became known as Muslims (Moslems)-Arabic for "the submitting ones". It was during this same era of time that Mohammed escaped from Mecca and from his enemies and went to Medina (also known as the *Hegira*).

Basically, the monotheistic formula which makes up the Islamic faith is, "There is no god but Allah, and Mohammed is His prophet." Islam contains the basic concepts of Judaism, Christianity, Persian Magianism and Zoroastrianism. The sacred books of Islam are the Pentateuch (first five books of the Jewish and Christian Bibles), the Psalms (Old Testament/Tehillim), the Gospels (New Testament), and the Qur'an (Koran), which was revealed to Mohammed by the angel Gabriel, purporting to represent the final word of Allah (God) to mankind.

There are six concepts/principles that apply to the Islamic religion: 1) the Oneness of Allah; 2) the idea of the gradual revelation from Adam to Mohammed; 3) the definiteness of the Qur'an; 4) the doctrine of Angels (an inexhaustible source for Islamic superstitions); 5) the belief in the definite decisions of Allah concerning an unchangeable fate (also known as "predestination");

6) the concept of immortality or those who die fighting for Allah and Mohammed are certain to go to Paradise.

The most well-known of the Muslim people are the Sunnis and Shiites. The Sunnis, who represent the larger fraction of the modern world, are the preservers of conservatism. The Sunni branch was founded in 767 by Abu Hanifa, a Persian Muslim who interpreted the Qur'an and the Sunna (a codification of manners, customs and moral and legal traditions).

The Shiites represent the other leading group of Muslims. They attach importance to individual religious leaders and celebrate more festivals. The early history of the Shiites is obscure, but some claim the Shiite branch resulted not long after the death of Mohammed when the minority group disagreed with the majority's choice in selecting a caliph (successor). The Shiites believed that the caliph Ali was chosen personally by Mohammed, while the Sunnis did not.

The spiritual leader of Islam is known as the Imam and is recognized as a exemplar to be emulated. The Imam serves as a leader of prayer and worship in Muslim congregations. However, according to the Shiites, the Imam must be a direct descendant of Mohammed and Ali, the first Imam, and be sinless and infallible (a reincarnation of Allah himself) in his pronouncements on dogma and a sign of Allah's goodness.

The last Shiite Imam, Muhammad al-Muntozar, was believed to have disappeared, and will one day return to vindicate his followers during what the Christians refer to as the "End Times".

While the Sunnis and Shiites disagree on the fundamental concepts of religious leadership, the Islamic sacred doctrine shares mainly the same congregational beliefs which include: the revealing of Allah to certain humans, such as Adam, Noah, Abraham, Moses, Jesus and Mohammed.

Jesus is respected as a human prophet, but not as a Savior, as the Christian faith believes. And the most characteristic trait of the Muslim is submitting to Allah's will and to what Fate has decreed.

Today, the Islamic nation is spread throughout the entire world, with the majority of Muslims being located in Iran, Saudi Arabia, North Africa and Turkey.

"Judaism"

In contrast to Christianity, which conceives Jesus Christ as the Messiah so often prophesied about in the Christian Old Testament, Judaism is based on the precepts of the books of the Tanakh: the writings of Moses (known as the Torah), the teachings of the prophets (known as Nevi'im) and the writings of the ancients (known as Kethuvim). The commentaries of the rabbis, found chiefly in the Talmud (compilation of Jewish oral laws and rabbinical teachings), are also instrumental in the Jewish religion. Judaism was first introduced by Greek-speaking Jews to distinguish their civilization from the paganism known as Hellenism and thus designated the religious creed itself. The theological idea of Judaism is purely monotheistic and there has been no deviation in beliefs that there are other deities co-existent with the one, true God of Abraham, Isaac and Jacob.

While the rabbi is considered head of the church as a teacher, scholar or guide, no spokesman is needed. The religious institution of the Judaic faith believes all Jews, through prayer, have access to God. Emphasis is placed on the freedom of man's will and the theory of original sin is rejected. Supreme importance is attached to practicing a good and just life, ethical and righteous conduct, prayer and observance of ritual. In the United States of America, Judaism is expressed in three forms which commonly accept the unity of God, the dignity of man, the authority of the Hebrew Bible, and of rabbinic teachings. But, they differ when it comes to practices and interpretation.

Three Branches of Judaism:

Orthodox Judaism—stands fast on tradition which prescripts Jewish custom and belief; faithful to principles and practices as evidenced by devotion and study of the Torah; daily synagogue attendance; strict observance of Sabbath, Holy Days, etc.; and follow dietary laws (also called Traditional Judaism).

Conservative Judaism—modified and reinterpreted religious practices of the Jewish life in accordance with historic trends, without molesting the principles of tradition through contemporary conditions (also called Historic Judaism).

Reformed Judaism—a product of the Enlightenment, this branch minimizes rituals, narrows chain of tradition and emphasizes ethical monotheism of prophetic teachings; religious worship adapted from Orthodox Judaism to meet demands of contemporary life, frequently affected religious law and custom to contemporary judgment (also called Liberal Judaism).

Judaism is basically the sum total of the scrupulous philosophy of the ancients and the experience of the Jewish people, as expressed in their sacred literature and developed during the many centuries of their existence. Today, the religion of Judaism is practiced worldwide. However, the largest Judaism sect can be found in Israel and the United States of America.

"OTHER RELIGIONS"

Buddhism is the polytheistic religion developed in India during the final centuries of the B. C. era and was adapted from Hinduism. Buddha (historically known as Prince Siddhartha) founded the church doctrine in the 4th century B.C. His teachings, *Four Great Truths*, inferred the idea of the world being evil and only complete separation from worldliness led toward absolute divine being. Reincarnation is recognized and accepted in the hope that their consecutive reincarnations will be met on a higher level.

There are various sects of Buddhism that differ essentially. Some believe virtuous life and serious thinking is sufficient. Others maintain meditation develops supernatural powers. Still other factions believe supernatural intervention is needed to aid mankind, otherwise a virtuous life and meditation won't help.

The Tibetan Buddhist recognizes the Dalai Lama as the religious organization's spiritual leader. The Dalai Lama, who is reputed to be the reincarnation of the previous Dalai Lama and all his magistrates tracing back to 1391 A.D., was considered the "head of government" to the Tibetan people from the 17th century until 1959 when the People's Republic of China took full control.

The Dalai Lama fled to India and has since surrendered temporal power to the elected government-in-exile. The historic development of Buddhism ranges from an abstract philosophical system, which gained great influence in Europe in the early part of the A.D. era, to the crudest forms of superstition.

The difference between Buddhism and the Western God-fearing gospels is in its lack of a personal god and a religious creed. The majority of Buddhism followers can be found in China, Burma, Japan, Tibet and Ceylon.

Hinduism is basically an ancient religion known as "Brahmanism". It is best defined as a complexity of all religious ideas of India. The original polytheistic religious philosophy of the Brahman was founded about 2500 B.C. and Hinduism surfaced in the latter portion of the B.C. era.

The Hindus believe in the transmigration of souls and their final union with the Absolute Spirit. It is believed that the Brahma (one of the Hindu gods) is the original existence of all individual souls. The Brahma can be divided into creating, preserving and destroying principles, as personified in the Hindu gods: Brahma, Siva and Vishu.

Hinduism has no organized common creed even unto this day. In the 19th century A.D., Christianity began to affect Hinduism and many religious sects were founded which reflected this.

The most well-known sect which emerged was the Rama-Krishna movement of the late 1800's. Between the most primitive and the most advanced versions, Hinduism has survived for thousands of years and is still a stronghold of a religion. Today, the majority of Hindu followers can be found in India, Nepal, Bangladesh, Indonesia, Sri Lanka and Pakistan.

Paganism is considered one of the oldest polytheistic religions in the world, with Paganism being theoretically traced to the beginnings of mankind. Residing closer to Earth's natural cycles in an ancient society accredited mankind an infinity with nature. From this union, humans began to personify the energies of the land as individual and independent gods and goddesses, such as the Roman and Greek gods of mythology.

According to researchers, they support a theory that the most ancient formalized 'religion' was one of "ancestor worship". The earliest evidence, which brings about the conclusion of the researchers in their theory, is the pre-Christian Roman culture that indicated the Romans once practiced "ancestor worship". The Christian, Islamic and Jewish Bibles have indicated that the Egyptians, Babylonians and Romans practiced idolatry during antiquity as well.

The word "pagan" (meaning *civilian* in Latin) came about after the death of Jesus Christ and the term originally designated all non-Christians, such as the Muslims and Jews. However, this example was commonly used during the Crusades, and has been since modified to exclude the Muslims and Jews. The modern sense of the term "pagan" usually refers to idolaters, heathens, believers in primitive and ancient religions and irreligious persons. Paganism has been linked to Voodoo, Native American rituals, Satanism, and various other polytheistic religious creeds.

Paganism, most definitely still in practice, is a more low-keyed religion in today's modern world and mainly recognized in China, the United States, Continental and Latin Europe, as well as various other locations around the world.

Satanism is invariably a new and modern religion, but the concept of Satanism has evolved over many centuries and dates back to the ancient religious custom of Setianism. This is associated with the Egyptian god, Set, who [some believe] is in connection with the biblical Satan.

The word "satanism" commonly refers to the "worship of Satan or the powers of Evil", but the term can refer to a variable belief system, depending on the individual and the contexts used. There are three (3) common branches co-occurrent with Satanism: LaVeyan Satanism, Theistic Satanism and Philosophical Satanism.

LaVeyan Satanism, considered the largest Satanist religious organization in the world, was organized by Anton Szandor LaVey in 1966 A.D. and considered the "first carnal religion in human history". The teachings of LaVey are based on individualism, self-indulgence, and the "eye for an eye" concept of morality. The religion does not literally worship Satan, but uses Satan as a symbol for people's inner desires and lusts. Rituals and magic are also used.

Theistic Satanism is a general term for the forms of Satanism which believe that Satan is an actual deity and/or supreme force. They are not atheists and most believe in a cognizant universe. Great emphasis is placed upon the serpent (snake)—believed to be one of the many incarnations of Satan—in the book of Genesis. The basic teachings include being blessed with the "forbidden" fruit of knowledge, which brings about the birth of wisdom, and the actual worshiping of Satan.

Philosophical Satanism is a small religious group that is unrelated to any other faith or religious creed. They do not worship Satan as the Theistic Satanist, but merely uses Satan as a concept to explain their purpose of opposing religion of any kind. Common morals are followed, like that of the LaVeyan follower, and certain practices and rituals are instituted, such as: Astrology (for predicting the future); Alchemy (for finding cures for diseases); Astral Travel (out of body experiences); and Spiritualism (pagan practice of talking with the dead).

Satanism, while virtually a new form of a religious creed in our modern times, has many followers scattered throughout the entire world. In the 1970's, it was estimated that the Church of Satan had 10,000 to 20,000 members in the United States. In 1987, the Church of Satan had an estimated 1,000,000 members in America. As the church does not release its membership totals, it is impossible to get accurate data for this movement.

Taoism is a form of ancient religious worship derived from the teachings of Lao-tse, a Chinese philosopher of the 6th century B.C. Some scholars believe Taoism has existed since the prehistoric era, but no credible documentation exists prior to Lao-tse, who was credited with giving the religion a written form.

The holy book attributed to Lao-tse, *The Tao The King* (the Teaching of Tao), propounded a religious doctrine called Tao (the Way), which ultimately led to the forming of Taoism. The religious creed's central point is the universe operates in its own way. It also states that mankind should align themselves in the same way in order to achieve happiness.

In contrast to Confucius—who expounded upon authority and piety—Lao-tse stressed ethical perfection of the individual. Some scholars believe that Lao-tse was a teacher of Confucius, because many of the ancient scholar's ideas were gradually incorporated into Confucianism.

The teaching of Confucius dictates the highest possible ethical concepts, which contains the virtues of wisdom, benevolence, courage, righteousness, propriety and good faith. Today, Taoism is primarily practiced in Taiwan, China and various Asian countries.

While the various religions of the world share some similarities and dispute others, the atheists stand alone in their united belief that no supreme deity/deities exist. In Western culture the majority of the atheists are irreligious, with the minority of non-believers being spiritual.

These minority atheists practice certain religious and spiritual belief systems such as Buddhism, Hinduism and Paganism [i.e. Wicca]. It is hard to determine how many atheists exist in the 21st century, but estimates put it close to 2.3% of the world's population.

"THE HOLY BOOKS OF THE WORLD"

When referring to religion it can be defined very broadly. Thus, the religious books in the world can also be similarly circumscribed. There are many Holy Books today that contain specific systems of beliefs, codes of ethics and philosophies of life. In almost every religion around the world, the congregation depends on a Holy Book.

Many times these Holy Books are attributed to the Creator or various gods and some believe divine inspiration was involved. The skeptics, however, contend that all books were written by human beings and being inspired of a holy book is likened unto being inspired by such literary artists as William Shakespeare.

Once again mankind finds itself at an impasse concerning the Holy Books that are circulating around the planet, especially when the majority of the world deems the divine books to be sacred. The following is a list of a few Holy Books in circulation today:

The Analects . . . a collection of Confucius' teachings that are thought to have been recorded and written by his students around the 3rd century B.C.

The Apocrypha . . . the 14 sacred books of the Septuagint (Greek translation of the Hebrew Scriptures) that was rejected in Protestantism and Judaism; 11 books are accepted in the Roman Catholic biblical canon.

The Avesta . . . the primary collection of the sacred texts of Zoroastrianism. These writings originated over a period spanning most of the 1st millennium B. C. and notably include the Old Avestan Gathas (17 hymns ascribed to Zoroaster himself).

Bhagavad Gita . . . a Sanskrit poem, written between 200 B.C. and 200 A.D., that is part of the Indian epic known as the *Mahabharata*. It describes the Hindu path to spiritual wisdom and the unity with God that can be achieved through karma (action), bhakti (devotion) and jnana (knowledge).

Dead Sea Scrolls . . . a compilation of eschalogical writings of the Essenes (an ancient Jewish race) which were written and protected over a 200 year span from c/132 B.C. to c/68 A.D. The Essenes were wiped out in a great war with the Romans in 68 A.D. and the scrolls were hidden in a multiple cave system near Qumran prior to their extinction. The Dead Sea Scrolls were discovered by a humble shepherd in 1947 A.D. and considered the greatest ancient discovery of the 20th century.

Hadith . . . is mainly a collection of Mohammed's sayings (not considered revelations from Allah) and stories about the Islamic messiah's life. This holy text was compiled in 9th century (A.D.). While several authors are credited with compiling the Hadith, al-Bukhari collected the most authoritative sayings of Mohammed.

New Testament . . . is the second portion of the Christian Bible, which forms the basis of Christian belief. The book contains the teachings of Jesus, the writings of the apostles, instruction for converting nonbelievers and performing baptisms, blessings and other rituals. It is believed the New Testament was written around 100 A.D.

Old Testament . . . is the Christian name for the Jewish (Hebrew) Bible; contains the sacred scriptures of Judaism and is the first portion of the Christian Bible. The Old Testament describes the origins of the world, the history of the Israelites, the various concepts governing social and religious behavior and many stories of heroes, kings and wars. Scholars generally agree that the Old Testament was compiled sometime between 1000 B.C. to 100 B. C.

Qur'an . . . also referred to as Koran, is the primary book of Islam which contains impassioned appeals for belief in Allah (God), encouragement to lead a moral life, portrayals of damnation and beatitude, stories of Islamic prophets, and rules governing the social and religious life of Muslims. The authoritative text of Islam was produced around 650 A.D.

Talmud . . . is the compilation of Jewish oral law and rabbinical teachings. It is made up of two parts: the *Mishna* (the oral law itself) and *Gemara* (a commentary on the *Mishna*). This book contains both a legal section and a part devoted to legends and stories. The authoritative Babylonian Talmud was written in the 6th century B. C.

Tanakh . . . is the basic text of the Jewish (Hebrew) Bible, which contains the Torah (the law), Nevtim (the prophets) and Kethuvim (the writings). According to the Talmud, much of the contents of the Tanakh were compiled by the "Men of Great Assembly" by 450 B. C., although modern scholars believe the finalization of the canon occurred between 200 B.C. and 200 A.D.

<u>Tao te ching</u> . . . is the basic text of the Chinese philosophy and religion known as Taoism. It is a compilation of 81 short chapters and depicts a way of life marked by quiet effortlessness and freedom from desire. This book is attributed to Lao-tse, although it has not been positively proven. Some claim it was compiled by many writers over a long period of time.

<u>Torah</u> . . . is the first part of the Jewish Bible (Tanakh) and contains the sacred Judaic scriptures within the five (5) books (Genesis; Exodus; Leviticus; Numbers; Deuteronomy) believed to be written by Moses. The Torah also contains a variety of literary genres, including allegories, historical narrative, poetry, genealogy, and the exposition of various types of laws.

<u>Veda</u> . . . is the sacred scriptures of Hinduism. It is a publication of prayers and hymns that are considered to be revelations of eternal youth written by seer-poets and inspired by the gods. The writings uphold that Brahman (Absolute Self) underlies all reality and can be known by invoking gods through the use of hymns. The Hindu texts were recorded between 1000 and 500 B. C.

<u>Zohar</u> . . . also known as the Book of Splendor, is a collection of Kabbalah commentaries on the Torah, material on mysticism, as well as mystical psychology. The Zohar has a rather elusive history, possibly being in existence as early as 539 B.C., however the book was accredited to Rabbi Shimon Bar Yochai (Rashbi), who purportedly wrote it in the 2nd or 3rd century A.D.

In all religions, Holy Books are considered sacred and their texts are the central importance to their religious tradition. Many religions, as well as spiritual movements, believe that their consecrated writings are divinely or supernaturally inspired. Scholars agree that attitudes toward sacred texts differ.

Some religions make their texts available to anyone; while others hold that their hallowed texts must remain hidden from all but the loyal and just. Many religions view their sacred writings as the "Word of God" and not open to alteration. While the Holy Books of the world are intended to give mankind guidance and instruction, the ancient writings can produce many interpretations.

There are many people of faith who believe in an all powerful Omnipresence. And most are convinced the holy texts of the world are not only the Creator's instruction manual, but a road map leading to future events.

"SATAN & A HISTORY OF HELL"

When you read the Holy Books of the world you find missing pieces of the characters and places you know well and, in some instances, you stumble upon those who have names, but hardly a story is attributed to them. Such is the case when referring to Heaven, Hell and Satan.

During the centuries of mankind's existence, Satan and Hell have been explicitly intertwined with one another. The Holy Books of the world does not mention Satan often nor do the ancient writings expand upon a Hell. According to researchers and scholars of biblical studies, the majority of today's population believes that Satan and Hell do exist. Many modern theologians have found a basic denominator while researching religion: where there is good, there is evil; where there is a Heaven, there is a Hell; where there is God, there is Satan.

Satan

Many scholars of religion agree that Satan was the fallen angel, Lucifer, who was thrown out of Heaven for his presumptuous challenge of demanding the Creator's heavenly throne. Satan was defeated in the celestial battle for power by the angel, Michael and his army. Soon after, Lucifer was thrown out of Heaven, and to this day, has never returned.

The Christian faith believes that Satan watches over Hell and entices mankind to join him there. The Islamic faith decrees that only a few will receive the condemnation of Hell. While the Jewish faith denies the existence of Satan and Hell, Judaism teaches that sinners who practice evil deeds will be dealt with by the Creator directly.

Some religions believe the Creator gave Satan reign over Hell and in his dark dominion is where he devilishly schemes to avenge his fall from grace. Other religious congregations believe the perception of Satan's dark side was basically enhanced by mankind. The ancient pagans acknowledged that Satan was descended from Set, the Egyptian God of the Underworld and Pan, the Greek God who was half man/half beast and ruled over sexual desire.

The modern perception of Satan began with the early Christians of antiquity. The ancients felt the enigmatic Satan was a minor figure, not an evil mastermind. A few of the early Christians disagreed. They sought out Satan in the Old Testament and poured over many scriptures. Our ancient ancestors were convinced that the serpent (snake) in the Garden of Eden, the one who tempted Eve to eat the fruit of the Tree of Knowledge, was Lucifer in one of his many disguises. While Judaism originally introduced Satan in the book of Job, it was the early Christians who embellished upon the character of the Creator's foe (some scholars attribute this to Satan's tempting of Jesus in Matthew 4:1-11).

Eager to spread the word of Christ, these zealous Christian ministers of yesteryear warned of Satan's wickedness and Lucifer was formally introduced to mankind. In the 6th century A.D., Pope Gregory the Great preached that Satan had powers and attributed seven sins to him: 1) Anger, 2) Envy, 3) Gluttony, 4) Greed, 5) Lust, 6) Pride, and 7) Sloth. This would later become known as the "Seven Deadly Sins of Mankind". By the 10th century, Satan had assumed a monstrous form and some artists of the era captured an evil looking devil with horns and a tail.

During this same historical era if anyone opposed the Christian Church they became an advocate of Satan. By the 1980's the rise of Satan was more powerful than any other time in mankind's history. In 1987, there was over a million estimated Satanists practicing in the United States. Today, the concept of Satan and his evil powers continue in the various sermons of our religious leaders. As the Holy Books of the world does not say much about Satan, the details of the Devil primarily come from the poets, not the prophets. In all religions there is an equal balance between good and bad. Hence the birth of Satan . . .

A History of Hell

The majority of theologians and scholars of biblical studies will attest that the Creator did not cause evil to fall upon the world and mankind. Rather, it was Satan, who through his wicked rebellion, provoked it. And, henceforth, the Kingdom of Hell came into being.

During the first thousand years, Christianity did not mention Hell and it was rarely preached from ancient pulpits; with the exception of Augustine of Hippo, a 4th century A.D. philosopher. During an oppressive time of war, famine and plague, Augustine warned of the terrors of Hell. He was instrumental in helping pagan masses convert to Christianity.

By the early 1300's, Dante Alighieri transformed Hell into an ongoing story in his literary work, *Dante's Inferno*. The story, in which mankind struggles to understand the world, helped to shape our modern sense of Hell. Dante's lyrical literature had a profound effect upon the Renaissance era which changed the idealistic thoughts of Satan.

> *"Midway upon the journey of our life I found myself in a dark wilderness for I had wandered from the straight and true."* Dante's Inferno—Canto 1

Dante's description of Hell is very detailed and contains nine levels, known as "realms". Each level was designed for specific sins. The most vile of sinners found themselves in the pit of Hell (9th realm) with Satan.

As Dante forever expanded the notion of Hell, English poet, John Milton, revolutionized the character of Satan in the 1600's. Milton's vision introduced Satan as a champion of the "dark side" and a powerful deity in an adversarial role. The English poet produced his masterpiece, *Paradise Lost*, in 1667, which retells Lucifer's fall from Heaven. According to Milton, a third of the angels in Heaven joined Satan in his fall from grace. Satan rouses the demoralized angels and soon they became faithful and obedient servants to their evil master. John Milton also proclaimed that Satan cannot atone to God for such an insurrection, and therefore continually wages war against the Creator and mankind.

Many modern Christians of the 21st century believe Jesus descended into Hell after he died; not to save the damned or battle Satan, rather Christ went there to free the ancient souls from Sheol (the abode of the dead or of departed spirits) that were worthy of Heaven.

The Islamic view of Hell is not as detailed as the Christians' version. The Qur'an states Hell is a literal and physical place. The Muslims believe Hell was created by Allah to instill discipline and follow the truth. Those condemned to the Hell of Islam are greeted in a horrifying manner.

The pain experienced in Hell is intense, merciless and continual. While the majority of Islamic souls will miss Hell entirely, the minority of Muslims will descend into the underworld. However, Islam's Hell is not a permanent place.

> *"And when it is said unto him, be careful of thy duty to Allah. Pride taketh him to sin; Hell will settle his account, an evil resting place."* Qur'an 2.206

According to Islamic theologians and scholars, Allah's mercy overcomes His wrath and eventually removes the tortured soul from the abyss of Hell. Those souls, whose sins are brutal and horrific, will remain in what Islam refers to as Jahannam (Hell) until Judgment Day. Abiding in Hell could take a few days or many years, but in the end those Muslims worthy of Jannah (Paradise) will eventually find their way to Paradise (Heaven).

Judaism, on the other hand, has a different definition in accordance with the Christians and Muslims. As their Holy Bible does not emphasize an afterlife, the Conservative and Reformed Jews don't believe in a literal "afterlife" or Hell. There are some Orthodox Jews that believe in an afterlife and embrace the idea of appealing to God for a better station in the next life.

During the 12th century A.D., a few Jewish congregations come to accept the existence of Hell when Rabbi Moses ben-Maimon (also called Maimonides) penned a code of ethics that contained 13 principles of faith. Maimonides was considered a great philosopher, scholar and physician of the Middle Ages. The code of ethics, that are still practiced in our modern world, taught that reward and punishment still exist in an afterlife and the 13 principles entailed:

1- The existence of God

2- God's unity

3- God's spirituality and incorporeality

4- God's eternity

5- God alone should be the object of worship

6- Revelation through God's prophets

7- The preeminence of Moses among the prophets

8- God's law given on Mount Sinai

9- The immutability of the Torah as God's law

10- God's foreknowledge of human actions

11- Reward of good and retribution of evil

12- The coming of the Jewish Messiah

13- The resurrection of the dead

The concept of a Buddhist Hell, in comparison, is decidedly different than other creator-based religions. This religious faction believes that an "afterlife" is not a place, but rather, a state of existence. Hell is a realm where the dead are reborn into anxiety and despair.

The Buddhist has many realms or state of being associated with Hell, but does not believe in a divine judge who condemns man to Hell. According to scholars of Buddhism, it is one's own evil karma that gives rise to rebirth in this realm.

> *"He sees living beings seared and consumed by birth, old age, sickness and death;*
> *care and suffering cease them to undergo many, kinds of pain, because of their greed,*
> *attachment and striving they undergo numerous pains in their present existence and*
> *later they undergo the pain of being reborn in Hell as beasts or hungry spirits."*
> Lotus Sutra—3:37

The theologians also believe those who follow the light will have positive rebirths; those that follow darkness will have a negative rebirth. As in Islamic beliefs, the Buddhist's suffering in Hell is not eternal. Living beings suffer the pains of Hell until the unwholesome karma they had generated in life is well exhausted and soon after one is reborn into a new life. While the Christian, Jews, Muslims and Buddhists have a different perspective of Hell and an afterlife, all the religions have grappled with the concept of a place called Hell. Regardless of the dominant religions' differences, they all generally agree on a code of human conduct. However, the scholars, theologians and researchers of religion would agree that Hell of the imagination has many authors.

"RELIGIOUS LEADERS OF THE WORLD"

Religious leaders have been around since the beginning of mankind, and increase with each passing generation. Compared to the ancient B.C. era, the number of religious leaders in the world today is completely overwhelming and nearly impossible to enumerate. The following list contains quotes by renowned religious leaders of the world, both past and present.

Ancient Religious Leaders:

Abraham—c/2000 B.C. (ancient Hebrew spiritual leader & prophet)

> ❧ ▪▪ *"And Abram said unto Lot, Let there be no strife, I pray thee, between me and thee, and between my herdsmen and thy herdsmen; for we be brethren."* Genesis 13:8 (KJV)

Zoroaster—6th or 7th century B.C. (aka: Zarathusthra; Persian philosopher and founder of Zoroasterism)

- "*When you doubt, abstain.*"

Lao-Tse—4th century B.C. (Chinese philosopher and founder of Taoism)

- "*If I have even just a little sense, I will walk on the main road and my only fear will be of straying from it. Keeping to the main road is easy, But people love to be sidetracked.*"

Gautama Buddha—563-483 B.C. (Indian spiritual teacher and founder of Buddhism)

- "*However many holy words you read, However many you speak, What good will they do If you do not act upon them?*"

Confucius—c/551-479 B.C. (aka: Kong Zi; Chinese philosopher and founder of Confucianism)

- "*Heaven means to be one with God.*"

Plato—428-348 B.C. (influential Greek philosopher)

- "*Wise men speak because they have something to say; Fools because they have to say something.*"

John the Baptist—c/5 B.C.-c/27 A.D. (1st century A.D. prophet)

- Unto the Pharisees and Sadducees, he said, "*O generation of vipers, who hath warned you to flee from the wrath to come?*" Matthew 3:7 (KJV)

Jesus Christ—c/4 B.C.-c/28 A.D. (1st century A.D. prophet and founder of Christianity)

- Then said Jesus to those Jews which believed in him, "*If ye continue in my word, then are ye my disciples indeed; And ye shall know the truth, and the truth shall make you free.*" John 8:31-32 (KJV)

Ge Hong—284-364 A.D. (aka: Zhichuan; Chinese alchemist and Taoist philosopher)

- "*Where the Mystery is present, joy is infinite; where the mystery has departed, efficacy is exhausted and the spirit disappears.*"

Mohammed ibn 'Abd Allah—c/570-632 A.D. (7th century A.D. prophet and founder of Islam)

- "*O People, no prophet or apostle will come after me, and no new faith will be born. Reason well, therefore, O People, and understand my words which I convey to you. I leave behind me two things, the Qur'an and my Sunnah and if you follow these you will never go astray.*"

Modern Religious Leaders:

St. Francis of Assisi—1181-1226 A.D. (German mystic and preacher)

> ❧·· *"All things of creation are children of the Father and thus brothers of man . . . God wants us to help animals, if they need help. Every creature in distress has the same right to be protected."*

John Wycliffe—**c/**1328-1384 A.D. (English philosopher, theologian and transcriber of Wycliffe Bible)

> ❧·· *"There was good reason for the silence of the Holy Spirit as to how, when, in what form Christ ordained the apostles, the reason being to show the indifferency of all forms of words."*,

Martin Luther—1483-1546 A.D. (German theologian, Austrian monk and founder of Protestantism)

> ❧·· *"I am afraid that the schools will prove the very gates of Hell, unless they diligently labor in explaining the Holy Scriptures and engraving them in the heart of the youth."*

George Fox—1624-1691 A.D. (English Dissenter and founder of the Quaker movement)

> ❧·· *"The Lord showed me, so that I did see clearly, that he did not dwell in these temples which men had commanded and set up, but in people's hearts . . . his people were his temple, and he dwelt in them."*

John Wesley—1703-1791 A.D. (English theologian and founder of the Methodist Church)

> ❧·· *"The Bible knows nothing of solitary religion."*

Richard Allen—1760-1813 A.D. (American slave, spiritual leader and founder of African Methodist Episcopal (AME) Church)

> ❧·· *"This land, which we have watered with our tears and our blood, is now our mother country, and we are well satisfied to stay where wisdom abounds and the gospel is free."*

Joseph Smith—1805-1844 A.D. (American spiritual leader and founder of Mormonism)

> ❧·· *"How will the serpent ever lose his venom, while the servants of God possess the same disposition and continue to make war upon it? Men must become harmless, before the brute creation;"*

<u>Mary Eddy Baker</u>—1821-1910 A.D. (American spiritual leader and founder of Christian Science)

   ☙ ▪▪ *"The age looks steadily to the redressing of wrong, to the righting of every form of error and injustice; and a tireless and prying philanthropy, which is almost omniscient, is one of the most hopeful characteristics of the time."*

<u>Mahatma Gandhi</u>—1869-1948 A.D. (political and spiritual leader of India)

   ☙ ▪▪ *"Nonviolence is the greatest force at the disposal of mankind. It is mightier than the mightiest weapon of destruction devised by the ingenuity of man."*

<u>Bertrand Russell</u>—(1872-1970) A.D. (British philosopher, historian and atheist)

   ☙ ▪▪ *"And if there were a God, I think it very unlikely that He would have such an uneasy vanity as to be offended by those who doubt His existence."*

<u>Mother Teresa</u>—1910-1997 A.D. (Agnes Gonxha Bojaxhiu; Albanian Catholic nun & missionary)

   ☙ ▪▪ *"I don't claim anything of the work. It is His work. I am like a little pencil in His hand. That is all. He does the thinking. He does the writing. The pencil has nothing to do with it."*

<u>L. Ron Hubbard</u>—1911-1986 A.D. (American spiritual leader and founder of Church Scientology)

   ☙ ▪▪ *"But if a man were totally aware of what as going on around him, he would find it relatively simple to handle any outnesses."*

<u>Pope John Paul II</u>—1920-2005 A.D. (Polish spiritual leader and former Papal authority)

   ☙ ▪▪ *"The present-day mentality, more perhaps than that of people in the past, seems opposed to a God of mercy, and in fact tends to exclude from life and to remove from the human heart the very idea of mercy. The word and the concept of 'mercy' seem to cause uneasiness in man, who, thanks to the enormous development of science and technology, never before known in history, has become master of the earth and has subdued and dominated it."*

<u>Martin Luther King, Jr.</u>—1929-1968 A.D. (American spiritual leader and Civil Rights advocate)

   ☙ ▪▪ *"But today I feel that too much of the church is merely a thermometer, which measures rather than molds popular opinion."*

Scott Cunningham—1956-1993 A.D. (American author of Paganism)

&•• *"In Wicca, rituals are ceremonies which celebrate and strengthen our relationships with the Goddess, the God and the Earth."*

Current Religious Leaders:

Pope Benedict XVI—(aka: Joseph A. Ratzinger of Germany; reigning Papal authority)

&•• *"I did not expect it at all because for me it is evident that we come from the roots of Israel and the their Bible is our Bible and that Judaism is not just one of many religions, but is the foundation, the root of our faith. We share the faith of Abraham"*

Billy Graham—(American spiritual leader and adviser)

&•• *"The greatest miracle of the Bible is that the prophets of Israel could keep a religion as clean as a hound's tooth amid all the corruption and idolatry of the nations surrounding them."*

Harold Kushner—(American Jewsh rabbi and author)

&•• *"We have confused God with Santa Claus. And we believe that prayer means making a list of everything you don't have but want and trying to persuade God you deserve it. Now I'm sorry, that's not God, that's Santa Claus."*

Tenzin Gyatso—14th Dalai Lama (Buddhist leader of Tibet)

&•• *"Although I speak from my own experience, I feel that no one has the right to impose his or her beliefs on another person."*

Desmond Tutu—(South African archbishop and activist)

&•• *"Human beings are fundamentally good. The aberration, in fact, is the evil one, for God created us ultimately for God, for goodness, for laughter, for joy, for compassion, for caring."*

Daniel Lapin—(American Orthodox Jewish rabbi and political commentator)

&•• *"Jews need to understand that our safety and security in the United States is dependent upon the health and vitality of American Christianity. No country in the last 2,000 years has provided the same haven of tranquility and prosperity for Jews as has the United States of America and this is not in spite of American's being Christians, it is because of it. You might say that America's Bible Belt is the Jewish community's safety belt."*

"World Council of Religious Leaders"

The World Council of Religious Leaders (WCRL) was formed to serve as a resource to the United Nations and its agencies around the world in hopes of offering resolutions toward critical global problems through various faiths of religion.

The WCRL was launched in Bangkok on June 12, 2002 (A.D.) and its objective is to inspire men and women of all faiths to seek mutual understanding in the pursuit of world peace. The participants adopted a Charter that addresses key areas in which religious leaders can play a role in reducing world conflict and adhering to the critical needs of mankind. Their mission is as follows:

> *"The World Council of Religious Leaders aims to serve as a model and guide for the creation of a community of world religions. In the spirit of service and humility, it seeks to inspire women and men of all faiths in the pursuit of peace, justice and mutual understanding. It will undertake initiatives to provide the spiritual resources of the world's religious traditions to assist the United Nations and its agencies in the prevention, resolution and healing of conflicts and in the eradication of their causes and in addressing social and environmental problems.*
>
> *By promoting the practice of the spiritual values shared by all religious traditions, and by uniting the human community for times of world prayer and meditation, the World Council seeks to aid in developing the inner qualities and external conditions needed for the creation of a more peaceful, just and sustainable world society."*

The WCRL promotes and supports unity, as well as religious traditions. In doing so, this inspires and encourages the humanlike values shared by all religious customs to come together as one human community in the development and creation of world peace through a foundation of trust. The WCRL, with the cooperation of the United Nations, hopes to build a community where the world's religions can benefit one another, instead of being in continual conflict with one another.

~ ~ ~ ~ ~ ~ ~ ~ ~ ~ ~ ~ ~ ~

In researching, the author has found that various religions of the world could be considered the backbone of mankind's strength and power. Religion, in this sense, is a man-made ordinance for the self-preservation of humankind. Some believe religion is the embodiment of survival. In man's quest to reach the ultimate plane of understanding, religion becomes one's savior; in this respect, others feel it is wrong to identify religion with the expression of mere emotions.

For others, religion could be the testament of mankind's need for the recognition of the existence of a supreme being, regardless of its form and powers. This aspect reflects mankind's tendency to feel dependent on one or more superior beings, which is the common aspect accepted by the majority of the human race.

According to some theologians, the essence of religion can best be described as sharing a common belief in one Superior Being; a Creator who is all-knowing and all-powerful. Many will agree this is the common denominator of most all religions in the world today.

Any way one wishes to look at or examine religion, it has definitely gone through a process of development over the thousands of years of mankind's existence, and has continued gradually from predecessor factors and preexisting conditions.

PART THREE: THE "END TIMES"

"SCENARIO OF THE END TIMES"

For thousands of years there have been prophets and oracles who have proclaimed the world of mankind will one day succumb to a horrendous end, which will bring about the ultimate demise of the human race.

Various civilizations and cultures believe in some scenario of an "End Times." From the ancient Mayan civilization, who believed the world would end on December 21, 2012 (A.D.), to the modern Christian culture who strongly agree we [mankind] are living during the "End Times" right now, although secular beliefs vary.

While the Mayans once were a people of advanced intelligence, and many of their prophecies having come to fruition, most Holy Books state we live in a world without end.

> *"O Israel, that art saved by HaShem with an everlasting salvation; ye shall not be ashamed nor confounded world without end."* Nevi'im-Yeshayah (Isaiah) 45:17

~ ~ ~ ~ ~ ~ ~ ~ ~ ~ ~ ~ ~ ~ ~

> *"Unto Him be glory in the church by Christ Jesus throughout all ages, world without end."*—Ephesians 3:21 (KJV)

Some religions believe that a mere human mortal cannot predict an exact date for the demise of mankind.

> "*But of that day and hour knoweth no man, no, not the angels in heaven, but my Father only.*"—Matthew 24:36 (KJV)

~ ~ ~ ~ ~ ~ ~ ~ ~ ~ ~ ~ ~ ~

> "*Verily, the knowledge of the Hour is with Allah (alone). It is He Who sends down rain, and He Who knows what is in the wombs. Nor does any one know what it is that he will earn on the morrow: Nor does any one know in what land he is to die Verily with Allah is full knowledge and He is acquainted (with all things).*"
> Surat 31:34 (Qur'an)

The Christians base their beliefs on the "End Times" according to signs given in various scriptures throughout the New Testament of the Christian Bible which parallels our modern times. (i.e. Matthew 24:4-5, 27, 33, 37-39; II Timothy 3:1-5; II Peter 2:12; Jude 1:10 [KJV]). Today, there are many civilizations of people who have different thoughts and ideals concerning an "End Times" scenario, yet there are other cultures which are skeptical and question the authenticity of the ancient prophets' predictions. The following chapter gives one an insight into the various scenarios from the ancient prophets to the modern seers.

"THE ANCIENT PROPHETS"

In Western civilization, the most recognized prophets are descended from Abrahamic ancestry, and their histories are canonized within the Old Testament of the Christian Bible, Jewish Tanakh and the Islamic Qur'an. These ancient prophets were men who felt themselves to be personal representatives of the Creator and able to foretell messages in *his* name.

The sequence of the renowned prophets began around the 8th century B. C. They were men of vastly religious experiences. Their concern with the social and ethical standings aided in the growth of the Judaic moral teachings . . . hence the Talmud. After 800 B. C., the ancient prophets transcribed their messages in a written form to forever preserve the "Word of HaShem (God)" for future generations. In the Tanakh/Old Testament, there were sixteen prophets who left behind written documents for mankind to fathom out. The following is a list containing the Hebrew prophets of the B. C. era and a few of their prophecies:

The Major Prophets

1) <u>Isaiah</u>—the most noted of the Hebrew prophets. His prophecies (c/740) threatened judgment upon the corrupt and debased Israelites from both kingdoms (Judah and Israel) and predicted the captivity by Babylon. Later, he foretold of the exiles and the coming of the Messiah. These predictions included a magnificent future for Israel. His prophecies were made 500 years before the birth of Jesus.

2) <u>Jeremiah</u>—prophesied during the dark history of the destruction of Jerusalem and Judah. Later, he foretold that Nebuchadnezzar would bring a time of despondency for 70 years upon Judah. This ancient seer wrote with authority of the certainty of the judgment of God upon a sinful people, as well as the greatness of His love.

3) <u>Ezekiel</u>—started prophesying c/594 and continued his predictions for 22 years. His predictions are mostly in chronological order and contain three parts: 1} overthrowing the nation due to the disobedience to God; 2} surrounding nations being threatened with divine punishment and; 3} pertaining to the future deliverance of Israel and rebuilding their sacred temple.

4) <u>Daniel</u>—interpreted the dreams of Nebuchadnezzar. His prophecies contained promises of an eternal kingdom and foretold the history of the Chaldeans, Medians, Persians and Macedonians. His insights described various occurrences and happenstances of an apocalyptic world in the distant future.

The Minor Prophets

5) <u>Amos</u>—during 785, he denounced the corruption and oppression of Judah, using pastoral life to impress upon purity and freedom in righteous living. His prophecies were mostly directed to the Northern Kingdom (Israel). Amos taught that the future greatness of Israel was not to be sought through power and wealth, but to be secured through justice and judgment.

6) <u>Micah</u>—between 759-698, his prophecies flourished. He predicted the restoration of the Theocracy, the promise of forgiveness and forecasted the destruction of Jerusalem. Like the prophet Isaiah, Micah preached against the sins of his time and the horrid oppression of the poor by the rich.

7) <u>Hosea</u>—his predictions soared c/750 and compared the relations of Israel to God with that of a wife to her husband and the defection of the Israelites with a wife's adultery. The message of the prophet held a warning and denunciated the people for their idolatry and sins.

8) <u>Joel</u>—delivered ominous warnings about the time of Joash and, after the Exile, dwelt near Jerusalem. His insights were basically divided into two parts: 1} a great calamity caused by locusts; and 2} God's answer to the people's prayers. Like the prophets before him, he also foretold the Jews would establish a great nation in Palestine in the latter times.

9) <u>Habakkuk</u>—prophesied in Judah during the reign of Johoiakim. He was noted for his prophecies of God's retribution against them by the Chaldeans. The prophet also predicted the Chaldeans own downfall. He flourished with future insights between 630-590.

10) <u>Zephaniah</u>—lived during the time of Jeremiah. His forewarning consisted of a three part series between 630-624: 1} warnings against Judah and the Philistines; 2} the fall of Nineveh; and 3} salvation and a blissful future for those purified in the fear of God.

11) <u>Obadiah</u>—prophesied between 588-583. His predictions were directed against the Edomites (descendants of Esau) for helping to pillage Jerusalem with the heathen foe. As God's messenger, he predicted great doom for the Edomites and also enlightened of a time when the Jews would again rule over all the lands formerly under King David's control.

12) <u>Jonah</u>—somewhat of a rebellious prophet of the 8th century, he first ignored God's command to dutifully preach against the sins of the people of Nineveh. In failing to do so, God caused the ancient prophet to end up in the belly of a whale for three days (which was indicative of Jesus Christ's resurrection). Jonah's predictions included: certain territories would be recovered during the reign of Jeroboam (c/786-746).

13) <u>Nahum</u>—his predictions were directed against the city of Nineveh. His prophecies were divided into two sections which predicted the destruction of Nineveh. Little is known about the prophet Nahum, but some scholars believe he lived about 505.

14) <u>Haggai</u>—was noted for his exhortation to the Jews to rebuild their Temple. His book was purported to exist c/520 and contained four prophecies, all of them dealing with rebuilding the Temple under the reign of Zerubbabel.

15) <u>Zechariah</u>—foretold the destruction of Phoenicia and Damascus and the Jews passing a test of courage and perseverance. He predicted the glory that shall come upon Jerusalem after rebuilding the Temple, as well as prophesying that all people will embrace the Jewish faith.

16) <u>Malachi</u>—was the last of the Nevi'im/Old Testament prophets and dates back to 460-450. Not only did he see the Israelites returning to their old, wicked habits, but he vividly predicted a judgment to be delivered by a Messiah.

These ancient prophets of yesteryear, some from the Kingdom of Judah and others from the Kingdom of Israel, guided the people, as well as took part in local politics and national literature. Most theologians agree, that the Hebrew prophets set a standard for the way mankind is to live a good and honest life, but also to prepare for a future of hardship and evil.

During the Babylonian Exile, the prophets created the focus around the forces of the day and kept the Jewish religion alive. The seers of antiquity never tired of emphasizing the external hope of the Jews for the coming of the Messianic era.

Jesus Christ, the Messianic Prophet:

Considered the greatest prophet among the Christians, Jesus Christ is revered as the promised Messiah of the Jews. Jesus, who was proclaimed to be delivered of a virgin, was born in Bethlehem, Palestine around the year 4 B. C.: his birth is commonly considered a prophecy fulfilled by the ancient prophets.

His teachings and prophecies are canonized within the Gospels of Matthew, Mark, Luke and John (in the New Testament of the Christian Bible). The teachings of Jesus were mainly given in parables [moral lessons]. They were designated to express the truth by using comparisons and analogies. A few prophecies included a personal testament of the Kingdom of Heaven, his [Jesus] own betrayal and death, and a future apocalyptic war between good and evil.

At the young age of 12 years, his incredible wisdom not only bewildered and astonished, but terribly alarmed the priests of the Temple. Yet, it was his prophetic teachings and divine miracles that captured the attention of the Romans.

It was after the miracle of raising Lazarus from the dead that the Sanhedrin (the supreme legislative council; highest ecclesiastical tribunal of the Jewish nation between the 5th century B.C. to 70 A.D.) was forced to take action.

Caiaphas, the High Priest, foretold that Jesus would die for his nation in order to avoid persecution of the Jews by the Romans. Hostilities increased when the Romans felt the followers of Jesus Christ were becoming a public menace and Caiaphas' prediction came true when Jesus was crucified (c/28 A.D.)

Nearly 2,000 years later, his parables are still recognized and honored by followers of various religions around the world. Their contents continue the basic ethical ideas of the Old Testament, but increased them by changing the ideals of vengeance.

The deeds of Jesus were not intended to signify sensational feats, but merely used as proof of *his* divine nature and *his* mission in spreading the truth (of God). No matter how one believes, it cannot be denied the name of Jesus Christ is one the most well-known and recognized names around the world.

Mohammed, the Islamic Savior

Mohammed ibn 'Abd Allah (c/570-632 A.D.) is exalted by the Muslim people as its own prophet and "savior" of mankind. This representative of divine action was responsible for incorporating the Islamic religion around the year 610 A.D. after receiving revelations from a higher power [Allah].

Born in the city of Mecca, he was orphaned at a young age and brought up by his uncle, Abu Talib. During the course of his life he was a merchant, diplomat, military general, philosopher and reformer. At the age of 40, he retreated to a cave in the nearby Arabian mountains for reflection upon his discontented life and it was there that he received his first revelation from Allah through the angel Gabriel.

Not long after his encounter with Gabriel, Mohammed began preaching and spreading the word that "Allah is One" and that complete surrender to Him is the only way. This great prophet gained a few followers in the beginning and was met with hostility from some of the Meccan tribes.

In the year 622, to avoid persecution, Mohammed escaped to Medina. It was here that he was able to unite the conflicting tribes and conquer Mecca after eight years of fighting. His revelations from Allah continued until his death in 632 and formed the scriptures of the Qur'an, which is regarded by the Muslims as the "Word of Allah (God)".

At the time of his death most of the Arabian Peninsula had converted to Islam and he was instrumental in uniting the tribes of Arabia into a single religious order. While his life and deeds have been criticized by opponents over the centuries, he is revered as a true and just prophet by his followers.

What sets Mohammed apart from other ancient prophets is the fact that his teachings and prophecies seem to be consistent with history, even into our modern times. The Islamic nation, descendants of Abraham through the firstborn son Ishmael, does not believe Mohammed created a new religion, but merely restored the original, uncorrupted monotheistic faith of Abraham. They see him [Mohammed] as the last and the greatest in a series of prophets, such as Noah, Moses, David and Jesus.

Other Ancient Prophets:

Samuel was another great seer and considered the first recognized prophet after the 8th century B. C. Among his many predictions, one included the prophecy of the Messiah being descended from the lineage of King David. His book shows that a prophet belongs to a certain order or profession that develops progressively over time. After Samuel, schools for prophets-much compared to later Greek schools of philosophy-were founded.

In Eastern civilization, there were very few prophets, if the term "prophet" can even be applied here, for most all of the Eastern civilizations of the ancient era were polytheistic. A mere man was inferior to the ancient gods and therefore unable to foretell the future. Only a very select few (such as the priests and priestesses of Apollo) were endowed with the ultimate power of prophecy, with the exception of Zoroaster, a Persian prophet. He taught the doctrines of an individual judgment, Heaven and Hell, the future resurrection of the body, the Last Judgment, and life everlasting for the reunited soul and body.

He was responsible for creating a new religion (Zoroastrianism) in hopes of uniting the Persian Empire (which he did). Zoroaster, who lived around 600 B.C., abandoned the idea of serving the old Persian gods and, instead, taught that a single god (Ahura Mazda) ruled the world. Among his other teachings, Zoroaster inferred that the spirit of darkness and evil (Ahriman) was constantly fighting with Ahura Mazda. By living virtuously, one will reach Heaven, but those who follow Ahriman will be punished in Hell. However, goodness will eventually prevail, and the world will achieve eternal peace. Zoroaster's prophetic teachings formed the basis of the Persian Bible (Avesta or Zend-Avesta).

Today, the ancient prophets are not only still revered and renowned, but are highly respected and exalted by the Christian, Islamic and Judaic religions many centuries later.

"THE ORACLES"

An "oracle" is the term given to an ancient seer who was given revelations and prophecies straight from the gods (polytheistic) or the Creator himself (monotheistic). Many ancient and modern oracles from different races and creeds, as well as diverse cultures, have accurately predicted various events throughout world history, including seeing a final apocalypse for mankind. Several prophecies concerning doomsday have been circulating for hundreds of centuries; some of the prophecies have been fulfilled, while others are still yet to come.

The Ancient Oracles:

Oracles of Apollo—the most well-known of the oracles came from Greece, in the small village of Delphi, about 100 miles northwest of present-day Athens, near the Corinthian Sea and just south of Mount Parnassos' (Panassus) summit.

According to scholars, the oracle was inspired to be a priest/priestess by the god Apollo, and bestowed with power to see into the future. From the 8th century B. C. to the 4th century A.D., pilgrims traveled there from throughout the Mediterranean to pose questions to the priest/priestess. The oracle of Delphi would enter an underground chamber, surround themselves with clouds of incense and go into a trance. In this altered state, the priest/priestess would produce prophecies. The Grecian population continued to consult the oracles until the 4th century A. D. when Theolosius ordered the temples of the prophetic deities to be closed.

In 1998 (A.D.), geological teams discovered two fault lines running beneath the Temple of Delphi in Greece in which ethylene gas was produced. Ethylene gas causes a mild euphoria in small doses, while larger quantities can produce hallucinations, visions, and incoherent mumblings. Some skeptics believe the affects of this natural gas caused coincidental predictions and did not warrant justifiable means for authentic and precise predictions.

However, other scholars and theologians agree that the Oracle of Delphi correctly predicted: 1) the fame of Socrates, years before he was born; 2) the defeat of the Persian invasion of Greece in 480 B.C.; and, 3) the conquest of the known world by Alexander the Great. The oracle also foresaw a great and distant apocalypse of extreme measures for mankind.

The Sybil—an oracle from the ancient Roman Empire, who was reputed to live in a cave near present-day Maples in the 6th century B.C. She was respected by the noble aristocrats who would consult with her on everything from war to domestic affairs. It was said the Sybil would go into a trance and the god Apollo would take over her body.

The oracle from ancient Rome wrote *The Sybilline Prophecies* upon scrolls, which were housed at the Temple of Jupiter. A few predictions included: 1) the invasion of Italy by Hannibal (700 years before it happened); 2) the rise of Emperor Constantine and called him by name (800 years before his birth); and, 3) the coming birth of Jesus (20 years before his birth).

This particular vision of the Messiah was cherished by the early Christians. The Sybil also made dismal predictions of a distant apocalypse. She predicted the world would last for nine periods of 800 years each and the generation would begin approximately 2000 (A.D.) and be the last period.

> *"These things in the tenth generation shall come to pass. The earth shall be shaken by a great earthquake that throws many cities into the sea. There shall be war. Fire shall come flashing forth from the heavens, and many cities will burn. Black ash shall fill the great sky. Then know the anger of the Gods."*—The Sybilline Prophecies-Book 4

<u>St. John the Divine</u>—(aka: John of Patmos) was the author of Revelation [in the Christian Bible], an enigmatic book of warnings and words of advice. John received a series of ominous visions of an apocalyptic world while in exile on the Island of Patmos. The divine oracle foresaw such occurrences as: 1) diseases claiming one-fourth of mankind; 2) global warfare centered in the Middle East; and, 3) the rise of an evil world dictator.

Some skeptics believe the prophecies of the ancient oracle from the 1st century A. D. were in reference to St. John's own lifetime and most of his forewarnings have already been fulfilled. However, controversy arises in such a theory for John of Patmos not only foretold of a horrendous war, widespread death on earth and cosmic disturbances, but described happenstances unimaginable in the ancient world.

Whether you are a believer or a skeptic, the book of Revelation is one of the most controversial books of the Christian's Holy Bible.

> *"And the shapes of the locusts were like unto horses prepared unto battle; and on their heads were as it were crowns like gold, and their faces were as the faces of men. And they had hair as the hair of women, and their teeth were as the teeth of lions. And they had breastplates, as it were breastplates of iron; and the sound of their wings was as the sound of chariots of many horses running to battle. And they had tails like unto scorpions, and there were stings in their tails; and their power was to hurt men five months."*—Revelation 9:7-10

In the aforementioned verses, interpretations vary when it comes to the scholars and theologians, but most agree St. John is describing a horrendous battle among mankind in which the ancient seer tried to describe what he had seen and transcribe it in accordance with analogies of his day.

Today, St. John is one of the most noted of all oracles and considered by many to be a prophet and personal messenger of the Creator. His doomsday scenario, outlined in the book of Revelation, carries this sect's most powerfully prophetic warning of the End Times.

The Modern Oracles:

Mother Shipton—a renowned oracle said to have lived in the early 1500's A. D. She purportedly was born in a cave beside the River Nidd in North Yorkshire, England in 1488 and died in 1561. Her prophecies of a doomsday first appeared in print in 1641 by an unknown source. While some scholars find no evidence of her existence, nor any original texts, they speculate as to whether this Yorkshire oracle ever existed. It was Richard Head, a London writer, who made Mother Shipton a well-known prophet. Before him, her legend was passed on through oral traditions; the original author of the printed text in 1641 was anonymous and his/her knowledge was lost to antiquity.

Mother Shipton correctly predicted the defeat of the Spanish Armada in 1588, the Great Fire of London in 1666, and the arrival of modern technology. She even forecasted her own death. Richard Head, a literary writer whose career was wavering, published _Mother Shipton's Prophecies_ in 1684. Sources have been unable to detect how the London writer came by the 16th century oracle's predictions or if he actually made them up. Head could have easily turned the _pre_dictions into _post_dictions, as the predictions had already occurred, but it cannot explain how Mother Shipton's prophecies concerning a distant, apocalyptic world accurately parallels our 21st century.

> "_Around the world men's thoughts will fly,_
> _Quick as the twinkling of an eye,_
> _The women shall adopt a craze to dress like men,_
> _and trousers wear and to cut off their locks of hair._"
> —Mother Shipton

The common interpretation of this verse above indicates a likeness to the internet in the first lines. And it further describes the female fashion vogue of the 20th and 21st centuries. Regardless of the scholars and theologians skepticism, many believe Mother Shipton was unquestionably a real person and her predictions were incredibly accurate.

Nostradamus—the French physician and astronomer who lived from 1503-1566 A.D. and completed a total of 942 quatrains (four line poems) which he organized into centuries (groups of 100 quatrains). His family was of Jewish ancestry. Some say from the tribe of Issachar, who were reputed to read the moon, stars and interpret the heavens. But, the family converted to Christianity when King Louis XII decreed that all Jews renounce their religion and covert to Christianity or leave the area. Nostradamus' parents chose to remain and, as a result, Michel de Nostradame (Nostradamus) was born into a Christian home. A qualified doctor of medicine, an adviser to the Queen of France (Catherine de' Medicis) and a writer of philosophical treaties, Nostradamus was considered an imposing man of his time and influenced world events before and after his death. This oracle of the Renaissance was best remembered for his book, _Les Propheties de M. Nostradamus_, which appeared in 1555.

It is believed by many that Nostradamus made such predictions as: 1) the fall of the House of Valois (the deaths of the Queen's children); 2) change from the Julian calendar (of Nostradamus' time) to the Gregorian calendar (still in use today); 3) the rise and fall of Napoleon; 4) Hitler and Mussolini uniting as allies during World War II; and, 5) the assassinations of President John Kennedy in 1963 and Senator Robert Kennedy in 1968.

While some skeptics argue that Nostradamus' writings are a jumbled mess of words without meaning, many believers are convinced this particular oracle saw 400 to 500 years into the future.

> _"The year of the great seventh number accomplished,_
> _It will appear at the time of the games of slaughter:_
> _Not far from the great millennial age,_
> _When the buried will go out from their tombs._
> _Long awaited he will never return_
> _In Europe, he will appear in Asia:_
> _One of the leagues issued from the great Hermes,_
> _And he will grow over all the Kings of the East."_ (Century X/Quatrains 74 & 75)

Many interpretations are forthcoming when deciphering the works of Nostradamus, but these particular quatrains just seem to fit in with the "End Times" scenario. The "games of slaughter" could refer to the radical Islamic suicide bombers; buried will go out from their tombs—this is prophesied about in the Christian Bible (I Corinthians 15:52$_{[KJV]}$); quatrain 75 could infer the rise of a world leader whom will have much power over all nations (Revelation 17:12-13$_{[KJV]}$).

Black Elk—(1863-1950 A.D.) was a Native American holy man from the Lakota (Oglala) Sioux tribe who made ominous predictions in the 1890's. As an adult, he participated in battles at Little Big Horn (1876) and at Wounded Knee (1890). Black Elk was a cousin to the famous chief and holy man, Crazy Horse. He traveled abroad with Buffalo Bill to France, Italy and England.

Black Elk never learned the English language, which makes this prophet quite the interesting seer. This particular Native American oracle had visions (as early as nine years old) that his people would suffer defeat and be destroyed.

Another, more terrifying, vision included an apocalypse for all mankind. Such an insight produced horrifying visions of people screaming and dying, the land war-ravaged, humanity becoming animalistic and killing their neighbors.

Black Elk's prophecies brought about a movement called the "Ghost Dance" in hopes that the Lakota nation would be restored to its former glory. However, the U. S. Army misinterpreted the movement as an Indian uprising and totally wiped out the Ghost Dancers in the mid-to-late 1890's. This action resulted in bringing an end to this particular band of Sioux Indians, just as Black Elk had predicted.

The Lakota nation never again was restored to its former glory. Instead, his people were moved onto a reservation and there resides even unto this day, as Black Elk foretold.

> *"Grown men can learn from very little children for the hearts of little children are pure. Therefore, the Great Spirit may show to them many things which older people miss."*-Black Elk

The ancient oracles made predictions of future events, born of divine inspiration, that were remarkably precise. Many of the prophecies, foretold by the seers of antiquity, seem to have been fulfilled in the last 100 years. This could explain why the Christians await Jesus' second coming, the Muslims watch for the return of their savior, Mohammed, and the Jewish nation still prays for the appearance of their long-awaited Messiah.

"MYSTERIES AND MIRACLES"

When it comes to the enigma of biblical mysteries, the holy books of the world are filled with many stories untold. Generations of great scholars and scientists have tried to uncover that which is otherwise unfathomable. It becomes controversial in context, with the end results continuing to remain hidden in obscurity.

The phenomena of sacred miracles are the greatest mysteries of the Christian's Bible. They are well documented and, according to the majority of religious orders, brought about by the volition of the Creator. In this respect, the majority of the scientific community continues grasping the meaning of such concepts as miracles, when it is often impossible to authenticate "divine intervention."

While science needs some form of basic proof to discern and authenticate miracles, those who are believers through their faith accept that a "higher power" interposes and impacts their purpose to control nature's ordinary movements.

Throughout the timeline of mankind there have been mysteries and miracles occurring with each new, passing generation. The following is a partial list, from Genesis to the Gospels of the Apostles, of the mysteries and miracles recorded in the Christian Bible (King James Version):

Old Testament

1) Creation of the world and mankind (Genesis 1:1-27)

2) Mention of "Sons of God" and "Daughters of Men" (Genesis 6:1-4)

3) Giants roaming the earth (Genesis 6:4)

4) Mankind living to be more than 900 years old (Genesis)

5) The Great Flood that deluged the earth (Genesis 7-8)

6) Confusion of languages at Babel (Genesis 11:1-9)

7) Lot's wife turn into a "pillar of salt" (Genesis 19:26)

8) The ten plagues of Egypt; the parting of the Red Sea (Exodus 14:21-31)

9) Manna (bread from Heaven) sent daily, except on the Sabbath, to Israelites while in the wilderness (Exodus 16:14-35)

10) Nadab and Abihu, sons of Aaron, consumed by fire for offering the God of Abraham "strange fire" (Leviticus 10:1)

11) Balaam's ass speaks (Numbers 22:21-35)

12) The River Jordan divided by Elijah and Elisha near Jericho (II Kings 2:7-8 & 14)

13) A hundred men fed at Gilgal with only 20 loaves of bread (II Kings 4:42-44)

14) Daniel saved in the lion's den (Daniel 6:16-23)

New Testament

1) The conception of Jesus by the Holy Ghost (Luke 1:35)

2) Miraculous drought of fishes (Luke 5:4-11)

3) The water made into wine (John 2:1-11)

4) A man born blind is cured (John 9:1-7)

5) Lazarus raised from the dead (John 11:38-44)

6) The tempest (storm) is stilled (Matthew 8:23; Mark 4:37; Luke 8:22)

7) Jesus walked on the Sea (Matthew 14:25; Mark 6:48; John 6:15)

8) Jesus feeds 5,000 in a "desert place" (Matthew 14:15; Mark 6:30; Luke 9:10; John 6:1-14)

9) The transfiguration (Matthew 17:1-8)

10) The resurrection (John 21:1-14)

11) Peter and the healing of the paralytic Aeneas at Lydda (Acts 9:32-38)

It is interesting to note the first Christians were Jews and even they were fascinated by the mysteries and miracles of their ancient era, and having no written guideline [i.e. New Testament] to follow as mankind has in the 21st century, just accepted the phenomenal as the Creator's purpose in His mysterious mission for the betterment of mankind.

So many times the scientific community has the "practical" answer to these mysteries and miracles, or just refutes them. Yet, many religions are united in believing certain enigma and phenomena are manifested through the simple act of the Creator. The scholars and scientists are continually at odds with one another over the enigmatic concept of a superior power having control not only over the planet of Earth, but the entire universe as well. And, not knowing—totally and truthfully—is what contributes to mankind's curiosity and obsession with the supernatural and the unknown.

"SIGNIFICANCE OF NUMBERS"

Another great mystery contained within the Holy Bibles of religion is the consistent use of various numbers throughout the written pages of antiquity. Saint Augustine of Hippo (philosopher and theologian) wrote in the 4th century A.D.:

> *"Numbers are the Universal language offered by the deity to humans as confirmation of the truth."*

Some religious scholars find the essential key to understanding the design of the Creator's Word is biblical numerics. One such scholar was Dr. Edward F. Vallowe. He served as a Christian pastor in the states of Arkansas, Georgia and Tennessee and traveled America as an evangelist during the 20th century A.D. His ministry spanned a 60 year period.

Vallowe was steadfast in teaching the Book of Revelation and held many Bible prophecy conferences throughout the United States during his evangelistic career. In his book entitled, <u>Biblical Mathematics</u>, Dr. Vallowe wrote:

> *"Numbers are the secret code of God's Word. Only to the students of the Word, those to whom God's Spirit has given spiritual insight, will the code be made plain. God has been called the 'Great Geometrician' and is said to do everything after a plan by number, weight and measure. If God is the Author of the Scriptures and the Creator of the Universe, and He is, then the Words of God and the Works of God should and will [numerically] harmonize." (pg. 19)*

It has been suggested by some theologians and scholars of Christianity that many books of the original Hebrew Bible transcript were excluded from inclusion into the Christian Bible because of the significance of the numerology contained within the ancient writings. Other philosophers of religion proclaim the original Hebrew texts were written in three different languages and lost in translation and thusly when the Old Testament was modified into Greek, then Latin and then English, translation once again became questionable. The following is a list of a few speculated books lost to antiquity:

1. <u>Book of the Covenant</u> (Exodus 24:7)

2. <u>Book of the Wars of the Lord</u> (Numbers21:14; II Chronicles 35:26)

3. <u>Book of Jasher</u> (Joshua 10:13)

4. <u>Book of Manners of the Kingdom</u> (I Samuel 10:25) Also referred to as "Behavior of Royalty."

5. <u>Book of the Acts of Solomon; Book of Nathan the Prophet; Prophecy of Ahijah the Shilonite; Visions of Iddo the Seer</u> (II Chronicles 9:29)

6. <u>Book of Shemiah the Prophet; Book of Iddo the Seer</u> (II Chronicles 12:15) These books contained genealogies.

7. <u>Book of Isaiah the Prophet</u> (II Chronicles 26:22)

8. <u>Book of Visions of Isaiah</u> (II Chronicles 32:32)

Whether these ancient books ever existed is up for debate. However, our ancient ancestors, who began with the lineage of Cain (son of Adam), put much precedence upon the significance of numbers. It is commonly known in our modern 21ˢᵗ century world that mathematics is the universal answer for everything. Today, mathematics is subdivided into the study of quantity, structure, space, change, logic, theory and, more recently, uncertainty. Numerology is a form of mathematical theory and deals with recurring numbers. It cannot be denied that various numbers throughout the Holy Bibles of the world are not only consistent, but recurring (i.e. 2, 3, 7, 10, 12, 40).

As space does not allow enumeration of all number sequences mentioned in the Christian Bible, the following is a partial list of common numbers mentioned often and the references inferred to make a parallel connection to the significance of the numbers.

Two (2)

- ➢ Man and woman created as a pair (Genesis 2:18-21)

- ➢ Two lineages of mankind in pre-flood ancient world—Cain and Seth (Genesis 4:16-22; Genesis 5:3-32)

- ➢ Animals collected in pairs for Noah's ark (Genesis 6:19)

- Isaac's descendants came through two lineages—Esau and Jacob (Genesis 25:19-26)

- Moses' descendants came through two lineages—Gershom and Eliezer (Exodus 2:21-22; Exodus 18:2-4)

- Jesus crucified with two sinners (Matthew 27:38; Mark 15:27-28; Luke 23:32; John 19:18)

- Two witnesses to appear before the second coming of Jesus (Rev.11:1-13)

Three (3)

- The post-flood world was repopulated by Noah's three sons—Shem, Ham and Japheth (Genesis 10:1)

- Abraham's descendants came through three lineages—Ishmael, Isaac and Zimran (Genesis 16:3-4; Genesis 21:2-3; Genesis 25;1-2)

- Jonah in the belly of the great fish for three days and three nights (Jonah 2:1)

- Peter the Disciple denied Jesus Christ three times when the Roman soldiers came to arrest the Messiah (Matthew 26:74-75; Mark 14:72; Luke 22:61-62; John 18:27)

- Jesus rose from the dead three days after crucifixion (Matthew 27:62-64; Mark 16:6; Luke 24:7)

Seven (7)

- God rested on the seventh day after the completion of creation (Genesis 2:2)

- After completion of the ark and all the animals collected, God sent forth rains on the seventh day (Genesis 7:10)

- Joseph interpreted the dream of Pharaoh and precisely informed the king that there would be seven years of plenty and seven years of famine (Genesis 41:16-30)

- Jethro, the priest of Midian, had seven daughters, one of which Moses married. (Exodus 2:16)

- The Sabbath of the Seventh Year-in which the land was to be given a rest—was commanded by God to be observed (Leviticus 25:1-7)

- The book of Revelation foretells future events with inference on the number seven: churches, golden candlesticks, stars, lamps, spirits, seals, horns, eyes, angels, trumpets, thunders, heads of the beast, plagues, golden vials, mountains and kings. (Revelation 1-21)

Ten (10)

- Ten generations between Adam and Noah (Genesis 5:1-32); ten generations between Noah and Terah [father of Abraham] (Genesis 11:10-26)

- Ten plagues forced upon Egypt during the days of Moses (Exodus 7-11)

- Ten Commandments given unto Moses by God (Exodus 20:1-17)

- Jesus' parable of the ten wise and foolish virgins and their lamps (Matthew 25:1-13)

- Jesus gave his followers ten beatitudes (Matthew 4:3-12; Luke 6:20-26)

Twelve (12)

- Twelve sons born to Ishmael—son of Abraham (Genesis 25:12-15)

- Twelve sons born to Jacob—son of Isaac (Genesis 35:23-26) considered the 12 Tribes of Israel

- Joshua appointed twelve men (one from each of the tribes of Israel) to pick up a stone from the River Jordan. The twelve stones were used to cut off the waters of the Jordan, allowing the Ark of the Covenant of the Lord to cross the river on dry land (Joshua 4:4-7)

- There were twelve minor prophets in the Old Testament—Hosea, Joel, Amos, Obadiah, Jonah, Micah, Nahum, Habakkuk, Zephaniah, Haggai, Zechariah, Malachi.

- Jesus had twelve Disciples (Matthew 10:1-4; Mark 3:14-15; Luke 6:12-16)

Forty (40)

- The Great Flood of Noah's era brought rains forth for forty days/forty nights (Genesis 7:12)

- Moses on Mt. Sinai with God for forty days/forty nights (Exodus 24:18)

- The Children of Israel [the Hebrews] roamed the wilderness for forty years after escaping from Egyptian bondage (Exodus 16:35)

- King Solomon (son of King David) reigned in Jerusalem, over all of Israel, for forty years (I Kings 11:42)

- Jesus was tempted by Satan for forty days/forty nights (Matthew 4:1-2; Mark 1:12-13; Luke 4:1-2)

It is interesting to note that certain numbers do seem to contain a strange element of mystery. While numbers such as two (2), three (3), seven (7), ten (10), twelve (12) and forty (40) seem to dominate the Holy Books, other numbers are overlooked. Or so it would appear. How many times do the numbers eight (8), eleven (11), thirty-nine (39) or fifty-eight (58) appear in the Holy Books of the world? Not often, or not at all. The Apostles wrote twenty-nine (29) parables that Jesus shared with mankind and that is certainly a number that does not appear often.

Regardless, the concept of numbers having significance is but another enigmatic puzzle contained within the sacred scriptures. As with all debates, the concept of a "Greater Power" controlling all universal bodies through a complex mathematical system is still a subject that cannot be agreed upon and therefore remains a mystery.

"Signs of the Times"

In biblical history, many prophets foresaw and correctly predicted various future occurrences that have happened during the existence of mankind. For centuries, religious scholars and ministers of the gospel have been saying that the "End Times" are upon us. Even the Apostles believed that Jesus would return, to set up His kingdom, during their own lifetime. Now, nearly 2,000 years later, Christians continue warning of the imminent destruction of mankind and the return of Jesus Christ. The Muslims stoutly believe their savior, Mohammed, is soon to make his appearance and cleanse the planet of its unholy and unworthy inhabitants. Even the Jews agree that their Messiah will purify the world after exterminating those who practice evil and are unworthy of eternal life.

So many prophecies have already been fulfilled since the dawning of the *Anno Domini* era, while other predictions have yet to be executed. It is interesting to note that all Bible prophecy revolves around the "Children of Israel" and the promises made to their Hebrew ancestors so long ago. An extreme worldwide interest rests upon this small, persecuted country. Most of the planet is intrigued with the current events that surround Israel.

Today, there are more and more of the Jewish faith believing in Jesus Christ and His message. More than ever before, in the history of the Jewish nation, have this race of people come to accept and believe that Jesus was indeed the Messiah they had waited for.

To many believers, the Christian's Holy Bible is a simple textbook. It has taught us where man has come from and how man should live in order to survive. It is also considered the Creator's outline of what is to come and what mankind should prepare for.

The Prophetic Signs:

Such prophets as Isaiah, Daniel and Jesus have foretold and forewarned mankind of incredible events that will occur concerning the "End Times". The oracles were steadfast in warning of a doomsday scenario, as well. For many believers of Christian, Islamic and Judaic faiths, some of the ancient predictions have already arrived.

While all three major religions disagree on chronological order, certain events and interpretations, they all agree an "End Times" occurrence is assured. The following is a partial list of prophecies that have already been fulfilled and some that are yet to come:

Wars and Rumors of Wars (Matthew 24:6)

For centuries wars have been fought, but in the last one hundred years or so, mankind has had more than its fair share of battles. There have been over 16 major wars since the turn of the 20th century A. D., which does not include the various battles and skirmishes fought around the globe. (20th century wars: Boer War, Boxer Rebellion, Russo-Japanese War, Turkish/Ottoman Revolt, Chinese Revolution, World War I, Russian Revolution, Spanish Civil War, Japan/China War, World War II, Korean War, Hungarian Revolution, Bay of Pigs Invasion, Vietnam War, Middle East Six Day War, Desert Storm War, Afghanistan War, Iraq War)

The increase in warfare grew considerably, if not astronomically, in the 20th century. Not one decade has gone by without a war somewhere in this world being fought. Not one generation has passed away without there being a battle to contend with. Mankind has definitely struggled through their fair share of skirmishes these last 100 years or so. To many believers, this prophecy has not only been fulfilled, but continues to escalate as we enter the 21st century.

Earthquakes in Diverse Places (Matthew 24:7)

The increase in earthquake activity has multiplied many times over since the beginning of mankind. Just since the 1990's, the scientists claim earthquakes have been shaking the planet in various places almost on a monthly basis or more. Then you have earthquakes erupting where they had lain dormant for hundreds, if not thousands, of years. The horrid tsunami of Indonesia (that claimed over 270,000 lives in 2004) was caused from an underwater earthquake, measuring 9.2, in the Indian Ocean; in a diverse place.

Supervolcanoes (capable of producing an exceedingly large explosion and a giant caldera) are scattered throughout the world. Many have not had activity for hundreds of thousands of years and in the last decade these giant, catastrophic volcanoes are starting to awaken (i.e. Yellowstone National Park). According to the website, earthmountainview.com, there have been over 1,000 small earthquakes registered at Yellowstone—some that measured at a magnitude of 3.8—just since the beginning of 2010.

Increased Knowledge (Daniel 12:4)

One cannot deny how advanced mankind has become. Since the 1950's, we have seen the invention of the television, spaceships and corporate computers, just to name a few. In the last 25 years alone, mankind has invented cell phones, personal computers and video games. Many machines (such as appliances) are used and utilized around the planet today. Our ancestors would be amazed at such luxuries we [mankind] take for granted today. Mankind has been bestowed with such an incredible intelligence, in comparison to the ancients, that many people of various faiths believe this is a sign of the "End Times" that was foretold centuries ago.

People Running To and Fro (Daniel 12:4)

Since the beginning of time, modes of transportation consisted of animals such as camels, horses and elephants. Mankind's own two feet have been quite instrumental, too! In the last 100 years, the increase in travel has skyrocketed. Today, man can travel over 24,000 miles per hour on his way to outer space.

Many scholars and theologians agree the world is definitely a busy place today: everyone racing around in their cars trying to get here, trying to get there; airlines are overcrowded with people trying to get there as fast as they can; the subways are non-stop as commuters utilize the system in getting to work on time. The list goes on and on . . .

Many believers would claim that the ancient foreseers were right and this is yet another sign of the "End Times" prophecy being fulfilled.

The Rebirth of Israel (Ezekiel 36:24; Amos 9:15; Isaiah 66:8)

On May 14, 1948 A.D., the nation of Israel was reborn. For over 2,500 years, the Jewish people only dreamed of this happening. Some believe that during the "End Times" Israel must become a nation before any further latter-day prophecies can be fulfilled. The Christian and Jewish Holy Books state the whole house of Israel will be revived (Ezekiel 37:11$_{[KJV]}$) and God promised to restore the "Holy Land" to the Children of Israel (Ezekiel 37:14$_{[KJV]}$). For some Christian believers that prophecy was fulfilled when Israel regained statehood in 1948. When Jerusalem was captured by the Jews in 1967, it once more fell under the control of the descendants of Abraham, Isaac and Jacob [Israel]. Many religious congregations are satisfied and convinced the "End Times" are definitely upon mankind.

Famine and Disease (Matthew 24:7)

With each passing year, and each passing decade, world hunger increases and new diseases appear. It is not only third world countries that are primarily starving, but many here in America, as well as other countries abroad, are coming to experience the meaning of hunger. It seems there are more and more droughts just since the turn of the 21st century. Certain authors, such as Al Gore, claim "global warming" is a contributing factor when it comes to droughts, which produces less food crops, which leads to famine.

The increase in diseases, in the last fifty years, has produced an incredibly vulnerable world today. It would seem there are new diseases manifesting with each passing decade. Some are temporary (i.e. Measles, Chickenpox); some are treatable (i.e. Cancer, Diabetes); and, some are non-curable at this time (i.e. AIDS, Muscular Dystrophy).

The condition of the world's treatable sicknesses and terminal illnesses are steadily growing with every new year that approaches. Many religious denominations claim this prophecy is not only on the rise, but definitely guaranteed to get worse as time passes.

Rebuilding the Temple in Jerusalem (Revelation 11:1)

It is said that when the third Jewish Temple is built, the time of the end draws near. The first Temple, built during King Solomon's reign, and the second Temple, built after the Babylonian Exile, have come and gone.

Some religious leaders say the plans for the third Temple have already been put into motion and it has been rumored that some of the more elite Christians have offered the funds for the rebuilding. However, the problem rises in the form of the Muslim Mosque (Dome of the Rock) that currently sits on the original site of the first two Temples. For fear of antagonizing the Islamic nation and causing an all-out holocaust in the Middle East, the Jewish nation has made no move in pursuing the building of their sacred Temple.

False Prophets and False Teachings (Mark 13:22)

For many centuries, false prophets have roamed the earth and spread their false teachings, according to the theologians of religion. These false teachers have deceived many with their articulate words and convincing actions. Some believers connect this prophecy with the many fortune tellers and psychics whose predictions can be quite convincing. Other believers find themselves fascinated by their foretellings—available through telephone, television or internet—that offer a glimpse into mankind's future.

As early as 1844 A.D., William Miller (credited with establishing the religious movement now known as Adventism) predicted the end of the world and the return of Jesus Christ within his lifetime. It never happened. Others connect this prophecy with the many 20th century cult leaders such as Jim Jones, David Koresh, and Marshall Applewhite.

The 21st century has seen a few self-proclaimed prophets emerge: Sergei (also known as Vissarion Christ) is a Russian preacher that has convinced many people to leave their jobs and homes and follow him for he is Jesus Christ incarnate; Jose Luis de Jesus Miranda, whose many followers are primarily Hispanic, is from Puerto Rico and literally claims to be Jesus Christ. His doctrine is simple-it is a religion that has no requirements except to believe in him and he denies the existence of sin and Satan. For many believers, false prophets and teachers are a factor not only in the ultimate concept of deceiving mankind, but ushering in the era of the "End Times".

Two Witnesses Preaching in Jerusalem (Revelation 11:3)

In the book of Revelation (the last tome in the Christian Holy Bible), it states that during the "End Times" two witnesses will be killed and resurrected. Most Christian scholars and theologians believe the two witnesses will be Elijah and Moses (two distinguished prophets of antiquity). These men, prophesied about by St. John the Divine, will be well-known prominent figures on an international status, and will bring many non-believers of Jesus Christ to accept *him* as their savior.

They will be instrumental in preaching the Word of God, and preparing mankind for the "end of days to come". In Revelation 11:3-12, it says that these two witnesses will be killed while preaching the word of God in Jerusalem and immediately be raised into Heaven. It is purported that the whole world will see this at the same time. Many who believe in an End Times scenario would say before the invention of cable television and the internet, this would have been impossible to achieve.

"Eschatology Comparison"

The three major monotheistic religions (Christianity, Islam, Judaism) have many prophecies regarding an "End Times" scenario. As the scholars would agree, these religions believe some of the predictions of the ancient seers have come true, while other prophecies foretold are still yet to come.

While some scholars believe Mohammed secured some of his ideas from the followers of Christianity, Judaism and Zoroastrianism, the concept of Islamic eschatology is extremely hard to piece to together. Muslim scholars of prophecy do not attempt to compare how events are related to each other. As with Christian and Judaic theologians, who disagree on the sequence of the "End Times" prophecies, Islamic scholars disagree on the nature of certain events.

However, the three religions are considered inextricably linked to one another through their histories because of certain common factors in their theologies. And, all three faith-based institutions feature many of the same figures and places, yet they are often presented in different meanings and perspectives.

Although the three major religions of the world are intertwined and defined by common beliefs, they differ when it comes to doctrine and practice. Even their sacred holy books are reflected by such differences.

The following excerpted chart, a literary publication of Contender Ministries, depicts a fair comparison of the similarities and differences in the eschatological teachings of Islam, Judaism and Christianity.

SIMILARITITIES

	ISLAM	JUDAISM	CHRISTIANITY
The purpose of Jesus Christ Coming	Jesus (Isa) will return to overthrow al-Daijal in the battle of Aqabat Afiq in Syna to confirm Islam as the only true religion.	The Messiah will defeat the gentile nations and restore the kingdom of Israel. Isaiah will be fulfilled and God will be recognized as the universal king.	Jesus will come to rescue Israel, defeat the Anti-Christ, judge the nations and the wicked in Israel, and rule over a messianic kingdom.
Who Must Experience Death	All people will experience physical death.	All people will experience physical death.	All people will experience physical death except those living when Christ returns.
Resurrection of the Body	Yes—all will assemble at the mount of olives to receive judgment.	Yes	Yes
Judgment Announced with the Trumpet of the Archangel	Yes-Qur'an 36.51 "And the trumpet shall be blown, and, lo! They shall speed out of their sepulchers to their Lord."	Yes-shofar will announce beginning of messianic era, gather the scattered exiles, and serve as a summons to the heavenly court on the Day of Judgment.	Yes—Matthew 24:31 "And he will send his angels with a loud trumpet call, and they will gather his elect from the four winds, from one end of the heavens to the other."

DIFFERENCES

	ISLAM	JUDAISM	CHRISTIANITY
Belief in Purgatory	Yes—called Barzakh	No	Evangelicals—No Catholics—Yes
Signs of the Times	Major and minor signs will reveal that the end times have arrived. (Surat 21.96; 27.82;43.61)	Ten signs will accompany the Messianic 'birth pangs' of the end times. (Sanhedrin 97b)	Beginning of birth pangs (Isaiah11:11-12; Matthew 24:5,6,7) Birth pangs (Daniel 9:27; Matthew 24: 11, 25:15; Revelation 6-19)
Result of End Time Battle	A 'Great Destruction' which destroys all but God, then a resurrection and recreation.	War of Gog and Magog, in which God defeats Gentile and establishes Israel in its kingdom over all the earth.	After Armageddon, Satan is bound and believers enter the Millennium. Following the thousand year reign of Christ there is a final battle with Satan.

"Israeli/Islamic Controversy"

The theologians of religion believe during the "End Times" the conflicts and controversies will increase for Israel, as that nation will endure persecution as never before. For many centuries the conflict between the Israeli and Islamic nations, as well as their practicing faiths, have been an ongoing battle for power. At least, that is how many scholars regard the "Israeli/Islamic" controversy.

These Middle Eastern nations are both descended from Abraham, who first sired Ishmael (by Hagar, the bond servant) and later begat Isaac (by Sarah, his wife). Abraham is the common ancestor shared by both the Jewish and Muslim people.

The tribes of Ishmael and Isaac (sons of Abraham) can be likened unto the first tribes of mankind—Cain and Seth (sons of Adam). As the Creator allowed His "godly" lineage to flow through the bloodlines of Seth, so does the "godly" lineage flow through Isaac's descendants (the Israeli nation). The "ungodly" lineage was cursed upon Cain's blood-lines and, in accordance to Jewish writings, Ishmael's own descendants were similarly cursed (the Islamic nation).

Another synonymous comparison, between the Cain/Ishmael and Seth/Isaac connection, is the "holy birthright" which was handed down through the younger son's bloodline, instead of the elder son, as was (and still is) the Hebrew custom.

According to the research information gathered, it would appear the unrest and tensions, which is a basic element of the controversy, has been handed down for thousands of years and continues on into our modern day world. Researchers, scholars and philosophers agree that the following facts are instrumental in defending the Israeli right of occupying the Holy Land:

1) Israel became a state in 1312 B.C . . . about 2,000 years before Islam.

2) After the land was conquered in 1272 B.C., the Jewish people ruled it for 1,000 years and maintained a continuous presence there for 3,300 years. The Arab rule, following the conquest in 633 B.C., lasted just 22 years.

3) For over 3,300 years, Jerusalem was the Jewish capital. It was never the capital of an Arab entity. Even under Jordanian rule, Jerusalem (in its entirety) was not made the capital. Neither has any Arab leader taken the time to visit the nation's capital.

4) Some 630,000 Arabs left Israel in 1948, while close to a million Jews were forced to leave Muslim countries.

5) The Islamic organizations of Fatah and Hamas constitutions call for the destruction of Israel, even though Israel ceded most of the West Bank and all of Gaza to the Palestinian (Arab refugees) authority and provided them with weapons.

6) There are 22 Muslim countries, not including Palestine. There is only one Jewish state.

7) Jerusalem is mentioned over 700 times in the Tanakh, but not once is the capital acknowledged in the Qur'an.

It is interesting to note the two societies (Israeli and Islamic) have both existed for many centuries. Today, the global Islamic population is approximately 1,200,000,000 (20% of world population) whereas the Israeli population numbers approximately 14,000,000 (0.02% of world population).

Put into perspective, one knows that the Islamic people far outnumber the inhabitants of Israel, but the Jews have thus far successfully defended their promised land for the last 65 years. The controversy and rivalry between the Jews and Muslims have gone on for centuries, and the author does not foresee that it will be resolved anytime soon.

> *"If the Arabs put down their weapons today, there would be no more violence. If the Jews put down their weapons today, there would be no more Israel."*—Benjamin Netanyahu (Israeli Prime Minister)

> *"Our enemies can deal a blow to us any time they wish. They did not wait for permission to do this. They do not deal a blow with prior notice. They do not take action because they can't."*—Mahmoud Ahmadinejad (Iranian President)

"BATTLE OF ARMAGEDDON AND THE ARCH ENEMY"

The theory of the "Battle of Armageddon" is based on many books contained throughout the Old and New Testaments of the Christian Bible and in the Nevi'im and Kethuvim of the Tanakh (i.e. Psalms 2; Ezekiel 38-39; Daniel 9:27; Joel 2-3; Zephaniah 1-3; Zechariah 12-14; Malachi 4; Revelation 6, 11, 16, 19, 20). Purporting to be the ultimate fight between good and evil, the "Battle of Armageddon" is another mysterious prophecy forewarned long ago by the ancients.

During what the Christians refer to as the "End Times," a seven-year period known as the "Great Tribulation" will ensue and mankind will experience a most turbulent world, one like has never been seen before. The seven-year tribulation period will herald in the "fight of all fights." Neither man, woman nor child will be safe during this era of corruption, murder and natural disasters.

According to some scholars, the Anti-Christ (an agent of Satan) will appear out of a global organization, such as the United Nations (UN) or the European Union (EU). He will make a grand entrance into a very vulnerable world.

This person will have the ability to convince many people to follow and worship him. The lies and deceit will be embraced as truth and salvation by many when the Anti-Christ, a suave character of charming persuasion, will be successful in uniting all countries through a long awaited peace treaty with Israel and the Middle East.

The Anti-Christ will rule for 3 ½ years and his world leadership will be embraced by many as that of a savior. Some theologians believe the Anti-Christ will be instrumental in having the third Jewish Temple built. His reign on earth will be viewed by many as that of an extraordinary and awesome leader. This is the first half of the Great Tribulation.

The second 3 ½ years will become a nightmare as Satan's agent takes complete control and makes the world his own. He will force followers, and those who were struck with awe by his wondrous person, to take a mark on their forehead or their hand which will unknowingly establish a commitment to Satan. Some religions refer to this as the "mark of the beast" (also referred to as the number 666). Any who deny or renounce him will be put to death.

Some scholars today believe a numerical mark is already being established through the products we buy (bar codes) and the credit cards we use (numerical sequences or lines). Other theologians believe the "mark of the beast" already occurred during St. John's ancient era. These skeptics claim the "mark of the beast" referred to the Roman Emperor Nero, a tyrannical persecutor of Christians, whose Greek name (Neron Caesar) was the numerological equivalent of the beast's number (666).

As the Anti-Christ rules over the world, he will speak blasphemous words against the Creator and inflict intense persecution upon those who do not convert to his sacrilegious ways. In Revelation 7:9, it speaks of a "great multitude, which no man could number".

Many members of the Christian faith believe that great multitude of people will become known as the tribulation saints or those who will be left behind after the Christian Evangelical belief in a "Rapture" and come to find faith in Jesus Christ during the Great Tribulation. The state of the world union will continue for the next forty-two months as the Anti-Christ is unleashed on the planet. Then, according to Christian belief, at the end of the Great Tribulation, God will send His son, Jesus Christ, to confront the evilness and put an end to the interference of Satan. At least for one millennium.

According to the scriptures of the Christian Bible, after 1,000 years, Satan will be released from the bottomless pit by the mercy of God. A second chance for the Devil to redeem himself to the Creator is supposed to be bestowed upon the angel Lucifer (Satan). But, that is another great mystery that has yet to be defined.

> *"Then I saw an angel coming down from heaven, having the key to the bottomless pit and a great chain in his hand. He laid hold of the dragon, that serpent of old, who is the Devil and Satan, and bound him for a thousand years; and he cast him into the bottomless pit, and shut him up, and set a seal on him, so that should deceive the nations no more till the thousand years were finished. But after these things he must be released for a little while."*—Revelation 20:1-3

In the teachings of Judaism, their arch enemy is known as Armilus, an Anti-Christlike figure that has many legends attributed to him. According to JewishEncyclopedia.com, he will be a prominent figure, such as a king, who will inflict major persecution upon both the Jews and Christians.

The Midrash describes him as a bald-headed monstrosity with one large and one small eye, deaf in the right ear and maimed in the right arm. Purported to be the son of Satan (according to the Midrash), Armilus will set himself up to be the messiah, even the Creator himself, and many Christians will believe him to be Jesus Christ. The Jews refer to the Christian's savior as the scion of Joseph. The Gospels of the New Testament will be accepted by Armilus and he will use it as his doctrine, bringing more Christians to his side during the End of Days. However, this does not last and soon Armilus kills off the Christians, including the scion of Joseph, when the Jews refuse to worship him.

When Satan's son is unable to convince the Jewish nation to follow him, he will rage war against them and send them fleeing into the desert. After 45 days in the desert, and the Jews unworthy of the messianic period die out, the angel Michael will appear and blow his trumphet which will signal the final battle is about to begin. The remnant of faithful Jews will witness the appearance of their long awaited Messiah, along with the Prophet Elijah, and march toward Jerusalem where the last war between good and evil will be fought and Armilus will be destroyed.

> *"And he shall make a firm covenant with many for one week; and for half of the week*
> *he shall cause the sacrifice and the offering to cease; and upon the wing of detestable*
> *things shall be that which causeth appalment; and that until the extermination wholly*
> *determined be poured out upon that which causeth appalment."*
> *Kethivum*-Daniel 9:27 (Tanakh)

According to the Midrash, the Talmud, and the Kabbalistic words of the Zohar, the Judaic messiah will arrive before the year 6000 [of the Hebrew calendar]. The Hebrew calendar of the Orthodox Jew dates back to the creation of mankind and the year 2012 correlates to the Jewish year 5772.

The Midrash states: "Six eons for going in and coming out, for war and peace. The seventh eon is entirely *Shabbat* (Sabbath) and rest for life everlasting."

The End of Days will herald in the the great Messianic Era-a time of global peace and harmony—that the Jewish nation has waited for these many thousands of years. The idea of the Jewish messiah ushering in a time of global peace can be found in the scriptural passages of Nevi'im in the Tanakh under Isaiah 2:4 and 11:6-9.

The Islamic religion also refers to an 'Arch Enemy'. According to the Hadith, he is known as al-Masih ad-Dajjal, which is Arabic for "the false messiah". This evil figure will appear in the world during the Last Days (per Muslim belief, approximately 2076 A.D.) and pretend to be the *Masih* (the Messiah). His entrance into our chaotic planet will happen before *Yawm al-Qiyamah* (Judgment Day) and he is likened unto the Anti-Christ in Christian eschatology and Armilus in Jewish eschatology.

> *"And when the Word is fulfilled against them (the unjust), We shall produce from the*
> *earth a Beast to (face) them: he will speak to them, for that mankind did not believe*
> *with assurance in our Signs "*—Qur'an 27.82

Other scholars of Islamic eschatology believe the Dajjal (literally translated means Deceiver) is a metaphor for the United States of America. They believe Jesus was a prophet of Allah and taught that Allah was the one true God. The scholars say those [Christians] who believe that Isha (Jesus) is part of a Holy Trinity is being deceived and therefore Christianity as a whole is an Anti-Christ in itself because it teaches the opposite of what Isha taught. And yet others believe the Christian Bible was 'corrupted' by the ancient deceivers intent on supporting the dogma of the Trinity.

Most Islamic theologians agree the Dajjal will produce an attack upon mankind and conquer the entire planet by military force, as well as seducing others with material prosperity. Many will be rendered blind by his power, which will cause them [Christians and Jews] to be easily deceived by his unholy mission. Numerous followers of Allah will become profoundly misguided and conform to Dajjal's doctrine as well.

The majority of the Islamic scholars and theologians agree that the Mahdi [the purest Muslim since the Prophet Mohammed] will appear and raise his own army, which will include Isha (Jesus). The Mahdi, who will lead a "spiritual jihad" in converting the Western world to Islam, will eventually defeat the Dajjal and become ruler of planet Earth according to Islamic law. Those who are non-believers during this era of time will either convert to Islam or be killed. The Hadith says "the sun will rise in the west", which roughly translated means Islam will spread throughout the Western [Christian] world.

Some philosophers of religion believe power given to this dominant world leader, known by many names, will arise because the Abrahamic religions have become impatient during their long appointed vigil of preparing for the coming messiah (Judaic religion) or the long awaited return of the Mahdi (Islamic religion) or the anticipated second coming of Jesus Christ (Christian religion).

"THE RAPTURE"

The Christian Evangelical belief in a "Rapture" of the Church occurring was first introduced by the Anglo-Irish evangelist, John Nelson Darby (1800-1882 A.D.), around the mid 19th century. Darby's rapture theory contended that certain Christians would be taken out of the world prior to the Great Tribulation and, subsequently, the Battle of Armageddon.

"I believe that predestination to life is the eternal purpose of God, by which, before the foundations of the world were laid, He firmly decreed, by His counsel secret to us, to deliver from curse and destruction those whom He had chosen in Christ out of the human race, and to bring them, through Christ, as vessels made to honour, to eternal salvation."—John Nelson Darby

Such a complex theory, as the "Rapture", has produced many pros and cons:

The Pros

The "Rapture" theory contends that certain chosen people (whom are reborn and saved through the blood and grace of Jesus Christ) will be "taken out" of the world as we [mankind] know it and be "gathered up" with Jesus prior to the start of the Great Tribulation period. According to evangelists, such as Jerry Jenkins of the *Left Behind* series, this particular doctrinal belief is commonly based on the following verses from the Christian Bible (King James Version):

"For the Lord himself shall descend from heaven with a shout, with the voice of the archangel, and with the trumpet of God: and the dead in Christ shall rise first: Then we which are alive and remain shall be caught up together with them in the clouds, to meet the Lord in the air; and so shall we ever be with the Lord."
—I Thessalonians 4:16-17

~ ~ ~ ~ ~ ~ ~ ~ ~ ~ ~ ~

"After these things I looked, and behold, a door standing open in heaven. And the first voice which I heard was like a trumpet speaking with me, saying, 'come up here and I will show you things which must take place after this."—Revelation 4:1

Literal meaning and End Times eschatology is attributed to the Evangelical "Rapture" hypothesis. Some believe the theory dates back to the ancients, while others believe the prophecy of "Increased Knowledge" explains their deductions concerning an End Times 'rapture' of the Church. Many Christian leaders, such as Hal Lindsey and Dr. Jack Van Impe, not only believe that the "Rapture" will take place, but warns of its imminent nearness. For this particular sect of Christian believers, they will continue their patient vigil as they eagerly wait the day of their final reckoning.

The Cons

There are other Christian denominations, such as the Catholic, Eastern (Greek) Orthodox and some fundamental Protestants, that disagree with the "Rapture" theory. According to the Catholic Church, there are a few problems with the idealistic explanation. The following drawbacks make it unlikely for a "Rapture" to occur:

1) The origin of the "Rapture" theory is relatively recent and does not extend back to the time of the apostles. Catholics believe such a theory would have been recognized by the ancients.

2) According to the Catholic Church, the Holy Bible does not teach a separate "Rapture" event from the second coming of Jesus Christ. The thorough study of scriptures does not provide adequate evidence to support the hypothesis.

3) Such a theory contends that Christ failed and was rejected. Catholics believe that Jesus was rejected by some, but not by all and therefore did not fail.

4) Being saved from the suffering of the Great Tribulation is not plausible. The Catholic Church believes those who are followers of Jesus Christ will have to bear the cross during those difficult times and endure the hardships in ways that others will not have to.

The Catholic Church is more concerned with individual eschatology. More focus is placed upon a Heaven, Hell, and Purgatory and the relationship between them. Standing strong in those beliefs is encouraged as opposed to a fixation with the end of the world scenario.

> *"This idea of a Rapture event in which we are saved from suffering and death is Christianity without the cross."*—David Curry (Christian writer and author)

Today, the "Rapture" theory is a very controversial subject and in constant debate among the Christian's religious leaders. To the believers, the concept of the Evangelical belief in a "Rapture" occurring is highly probable and definitely imminent for mankind. To the non-believers, such a far-fetched hypothesis is incomprehensible and, as a result, becomes dismissed.

"MODERN CIVILIZATION"

Compared to the ancient world, there are many philosophers and theologians who believe the modern world can be likened unto an abyss of malice, murder and mayhem. Today's civilization has few values and even fewer morals. Some researchers claim the standard of life in the 21st century has become a "dog eat dog" society. More and more countries are becoming combat battle zones; crime increases with each passing year; and, the increasing natural disasters worldwide are displacing hundreds of thousands of people yearly. Other theologians claim mankind's lifestyle has become tarnished with adultery and fornication, as well as covetousness and ungratefulness. Blasphemy and disobedience to parents fall into that category, too. The ancient days of Sodom and Gomorrah seem tame in comparison.

> *"But as the days of Noah were, so shall also the coming of the Son of man be. For as in the days that were before the flood they were eating and drinking, marrying and giving in marriage, until the day that Noah entered the ark, And know not until the flood came and took them all away; so shall the coming of the Son of man be."*
> —Matthew 24:37-39

With there being so many uncanny similarities, the modern world can be compared unto the days of Noah when that ancient society was corrupt, sin abounded and mankind was out of control in a godless land. No one believed the warnings of Noah; no one imagined the cries of a simpleton would create such chaos. Ancient humanity was not listening nor did they hear the warnings, and death became the ultimate price they paid.

Today, there are many evangelists and ministers of the gospel who agree the modern Noahs' of the world have warned mankind of an impending global holocaust, yet it would appear the modern 21st century civilization is paying no attention to such warnings either. Unlike the ancient historic period, Noah's modern descendants have had more time to prepare for such a catastrophe (over 2,000 years opposed to only 120 years of Noah's warnings).

> *"Having eyes full of adultery, and that cannot cease from sin; beguiling unstable souls; at heart they have exercised with covetous practices; cursed children: Which have forsaken the right way, and are gone astray following the way of Ba'laam the son of Bo'sor; who loved the wages of unrighteousness."*
> —II Peter 2:14-15

The modern world has made it possible to communicate as never before . . . via the internet and cell phones. There are some religions that believe dating sites, websites encouraging demonology study, exploiting child pornography, just to name a few, are easily accessible ways of creating new methods of adultery, coveted practices and cursing children. Many scholars of religion agree that the world is in a horrid state of affairs that are comparatively common to the days of Noah. Many believe the dire predictions of the ancient prophets and oracles are coming to fruition, while the skeptics choose to study further into scientific and theological research. Some philosophers and researchers believe such apocalyptic eschatology contained within the Christian, Jewish and Islamic Bibles was originally written to prepare mankind for the final destructive end of human life. Whereas in our modern society the dire warnings of the ancients are more or less left open to individual opinion and interpretation.

"The Seven Empires"

While there are many people of various faiths and creeds who believe in an "End Times" scenario and base their opinions upon individual views, the theory of the "Seven Empires" are also based upon personal interpretation and open for debate.

St. John the Divine informed mankind, through his visions, that humanity would be granted seven empires during their reign on the earth. "*And there are seven kings: five are fallen, and one is, and the other is not yet come; and when he cometh, he must continue a short space.*" (Revelation 17:10)

Six major empires have come and gone and, according to some intellectuals of religion, the seventh empire is currently rising. During the ancient era of St. John the Divine [John of Patmos] the five empires that had already fallen were:

1) Egyptian Empire—according to some writers, the history of the empire extends back to 3892 B.C., long before Noah and the Great Flood. The Pharaoh ruled the dynasty until the Egyptians were conquered by Cambyses, King of Persia, in 520. While Rameses II was probably one of the most well-known rulers (noted for his horrid oppression of the Hebrew nation), it was his successor, Merneptah, who was pharaoh during the exodus of the Hebrews [led by Moses]. The Egyptian Empire ruled the then-known world for over 3,000 years.

2) Assyrian Empire—was established around 1320 B.C. by Tiglath Pileser I, who expanded the dominion over western Asia. This empire was at its greatest during the reign of Esar-Haddon in 681, who further extended the kingdom to include Egypt and large parts of northern Africa. The Assyrian Empire is credited with dividing the year into twelve months and dividing the week into seven days. In 606, the fall of Nineveh (taken by the Medes and Babylonians) became the downfall of the empire. Sarakos was the last emperor of this dynasty. This ancient empire ruled for 714 years.

3) Babylonian Empire—some scholars claim this ancient empire came about before 2500 B.C., yet no documentation survives to authenticate the actual rise of this kingdom. One of the

earlier leaders was purported to be Nimrod (from the lineage of Ham, Noah's son). The empire's greatest prosperity included Assyria, Mesopotamia and a big portion of western Asia. The most well-known king of the Babylonian Empire was Nebuchadnezzar (604-561), who challenged the prophet Daniel to interpret his strange dreams. The empire flourished for at least 2,000 years and the world capital was Babylon the Great for 1,700 years. The kingdom was conquered by Cyrus, King of Persia, in 538.

4) <u>Persian Empire</u>—also referred to as the Medo-Persian Empire, was officially established by King Cyrus in 538 B.C., but was considered a nation as early as 708. In 558, King Cyrus rebelled against the Medes and his successive wars may have destroyed the kingdom's former glory, but it made Persia a mighty empire. The boundaries of this ancient dynasty included Syria, Palestine, Mesopotamia, Asia Minor, Egypt, Macedonia, Cyprus and Tyre. Darius III, who began his reign in 336, was the last king of Persia. Alexander the Great overthrew the empire in 330 (which resulted from the slaying of King Darius III) and made it a part of the Grecian Empire. The Persian Empire last 208 years.

5) <u>Grecian Empire</u>—dates back to 3rd century B.C. when Alexander the Great conquered the Persians and made his kingdom larger by annexing parts of Asia, Africa and Europe. While this empire attained its height of prosperity under Alexander, his reign was a short one (330-323). After the death of Alexander the Great the vast empire was divided among his generals. Ptolemy, most famous of his commanders, founded a dynasty in Egypt. In 279, the Gauls invaded and threatened the kingdom's stance when states rose in the West. It wasn't until 146 [and the capture of Corinth] when the Grecian Empire fell and became part of a Roman province. The empire endured for 184 years.

The established empire that was reigning during St. John's ancient era of the 1st century A.D. was:

6) <u>Roman Empire</u>—officially declared an empire in 31 B.C., it was a vast dominion as early as 753 B.C. The grand kingdom extended from the Euphrates River to the east to the Atlantic Ocean to the west, and from the deserts of Africa to the south to the Danube and Rhine Rivers to the north. Romulus (founder of Rome) was the first of its many emperors and the dominion remained a kingdom until 509. From 509-31 this land was considered a republic. Ancient Rome was completely destroyed by the Gauls in 390, but soon after rebuilt the grand city. Rome reached the height of its glory and became an empire under the reign of Augustus Caesar (30 B.C.-14 A.D.) The fall of the Roman Empire in 476 A.D. occurred when the last emperor, Romulus Augustulus, yielded to the Byzantium nation and brought about the great kingdom's collapse. Rome remained the capital under Byzantium rule until 800 A.D. when it reverted to Italy. While the Roman Empire lasted 507 years, the dominion of Rome ruled for 1,229 years.

These six mighty empires have long since come and gone. The last empire to rule upon Earth is commonly referred to as:

7) <u>Revived Roman Empire</u>—will rise out of ten nations and become a great one-world power. Many scholars and philosophers believe this final empire has been making a gradual entry into our modern day world since the mid 20th century.

Some view the United Nations (UN), which was formally organized in 1945 to maintain peace and security, as being the forerunner for the Revived Roman Empire. Others believe the European Union (EU), which came about through the "Treaties of Rome" in 1957, will rise to that great one-world power.

In the Christian Bible, the book of Daniel (7:7-8) reveals that the last empire will be exceedingly strong, as well as diverse, and consist of ten kingdoms (referred to as "horns"). Both the UN and EU are strong international organizations with much ethnic diversity among its members. While the EU consists of more than 27 countries, the ten nations of the Western European Alliance have a completely separate status as "permanent members." The other nations who joined after the permanent (or original) members have only an associate membership or observer status. Likewise, the UN is made up of ten bio-regions that have been established around the world. St. John's prophecy of the Revived Roman Empire states that the Anti-Christ will rise to great power from out of the ten "kingdoms".

> *"And the ten horns which thou sawest are ten kings, which have received no kingdom yet; but receive power as kings one hour with the beast. These have one mind, and shall give their power and strength unto the beast."*
> —Revelation 17:12-13 (KJV)

The last and final kingdom to reign on Earth will ultimately fall and evil will be obliterated. Then, according to Christian, Islamic and Jewish religions, a judgment day for all mankind will be conducted by the great Creator, followed by the Messianic Era.

> *"A good man out of the good treasure of the heart bringeth forth good things: an evil man out of the evil treasure bringeth forth evil things. But I say unto you, That every idle word that men shall speak, they shall give account thereof in the day of judgment. For by thy words thou shalt be justified, and by thy works thou shalt be condemned."*
> —Matthew 12:35-37 (New Testament)

~ ~ ~ ~ ~ ~ ~ ~ ~ ~ ~

"Every soul shall have a taste of death: And only on the Day of Judgment shall you be paid your full recompense. Only he who is saved far from the Fire and admitted to the Garden will have attained the object (of Life): For the life of this world is but goods and chattels of deception."—Surat 3:185 (Qur'an)

~ ~ ~ ~ ~ ~ ~ ~ ~ ~ ~

"The word that Isaiah the son of Amoz saw concerning Judah and Jerusalem. And it shall come to pass in the last days, that the mountain of the Lord's house shall be established in the top of the mountains, and shall be exalted above the hills; and all nations shall flow unto it. And many people shall go and say, Come ye, and let us go up to the mountain of the Lord, to the house of the God of Jacob; and he will teach us of his ways, and we will walk in his paths: for out of Zion shall go forth the law, and the word of the Lord from Jerusalem. And he shall judge among the nations, and shall rebuke many people: and they shall beat their swords into plowshares, and their spears into pruning hooks: nation shall not lift up sword against nation, neither shall they learn war any more."—Nevi'im: Isaiah 2:1-5 (Tanakh)

The prophets and oracles of antiquity forewarned of the "End Times" so long ago. Today, the scholars, theologians and philosophers (who believe mankind is currently living during the time of the end) continue to implore us [mankind] to take into consideration the Holy Books of the world encourages humanity to not only be aware of the signs of the times, but to diligently watch for them. In doing so, mankind adheres to the warnings and thus prepares for a great holocaust that will one day affect the entire race of humanity.

"And when these things begin to come to pass, then look up, and lift up your heads; for your redemption draweth nigh."—Luke 21-28 (KJV)

~*~*~*~*~ Mankind *~*~*~*~*~

"The reproduction of mankind is a great marvel and mystery. Had God consulted me in the matter, I should have advised him to continue the generation of the species by fashioning them out of clay."—Martin Luther (1483-1546)

~*~*~*~*~ Religions *~*~*~*~*~

"I believe in the fundamental Truth of all the great religions of the world. I believe that they are all God given. I came to the conclusion long ago . . . that all religions were true and also that all had some error in them."
—Mahatma Gandhi (1869-1948)

~*~*~*~*~ End Times *~*~*~*~*~

"Nor let it disturb you, dearest brethren, if with some, in these last times, either an uncertain faith is wavering, or a fear of God without religion is vacillating, or a peaceable concord does not continue. These things have been foretold as about to happen in the end of the world; and it was predicted by the voice of the Lord, and by the testimony of the apostles, that now that the world is failing, and the Antichrist is drawing near, everything good shall fail, but evil and adverse things shall prosper."—Cyprian, Bishop of Carthage (c/200-258 A.D.)

BIBLIOGRAPHY

Books and Other Literature

"A Theory of Creation, A Response to the Pretense that No Creation Theory Exists" by Timothy Wallace (2000)

"A Treasury of Biblical Quotations" edited by Lester V. Berrey (1948)

"An Inconvenient Truth (the crisis of global warming)" by Al Gore (2007 Revised Edition)

"America the Beautiful: In the Words of Henry David Thoreau" by the Editors of Country Beautiful (1966)

"Genetics and the Origins of Species" by Theodosius Dobzhansky (1937)

Holy Bible (King James Version) (1972)

Holy Bible (Gideons International Version) (1985)

"Israel's Final Holocaust" by Dr. Jack Van Impe with Roger F. Campbell (1979)

"On the Origins of Species by Means of Natural Selection" by Charles Darwin (1859)

"The Life and Teachings of Jesus (According to the Earliest Records)" by Charles Foster Kent (1913)

"Vestiges of the Natural History of Creation" (Anonmyous) (1844)

"Who's Who in the Bible" by Reader's Digest (1994)

World University Encyclopedia (1968)

Websites

agapebiblestudy.com

arabicbible.com

atheistperspective.net

BibleGateway.com

biblestudy.org

bibleverses.com

BrainyQuote.com

brittanica.com

bscs.org

cftech.com

chabad.org

christianworldviewofhistoryandculture.com

christnotes.org

churchofsatan.com

contenderministries.org

countdown.org

csustan.edu

dictionary.com

earthmountainview.com

etsu.edu

evidenceandanswers.org

fordham.edu

freerepublic.com

hinduismfacts.org

Idolphin.org

inreach.com

inspiredbooks.com

jewfaq.org

jewishencyclopedia.com

jewishvirtuallibrary.org

liferesearchuniversal.com

localhistories.org

luminarium.org

merriam-webster.com

millenniumpeacesummit.com

motherearthtravel.com

newadvent.org

nostradamus.org

nwcreation.net

obie3.homesite.net

pbs.org

quotationspage.com

quranicstudies.com

religionfacts.com

spaceandmotion.com

spacetoday.org/Rockets/X_Prize.html

thinkexist.com

ucmp.berkeley.edu

Wikipedia.org

wyps.org

Glossary

A

Ahriman . . . the antagonist who is a spirit of darkness and evil in Zoroastrianism.

Ahura Mazda . . . considered a wise god or the supreme being represented as a deity of goodness and light in Zoroastrianism.

Allah . . . the Islamic name for the Creator (God).

ancestor worship . . . a pagan custom of venerating deceased ancestors who are considered still a part of the family and whose spirits are believed to have the power to intervene in the affairs of the living.

Anti-Christ . . . a great antagonist (one who denies and opposes Christ) expected to fill the world with wickedness but to be eventually conquered forever by the Creator.

antiquity . . . matters relating or pertaining to the life or culture of ancient times.

apocalypse . . . prophetic revelation about the expectation of an imminent cosmic cataclysm in which God destroys the powers of evil.

Apocrypha . . . early Christian writings that were not included in the New Testament, however the writings were accepted and included in the Septuagint and Vulgate.

apostle . . . one of authority sent out to preach the gospel and originally made up of the ancient twelve (12) disciples of Jesus Christ.

Apostle's Creed . . . a statement of belief ascribed to the twelve (12) apostles of Christianity and still commonly used in public worship.

archangel . . . a chief angel or an entire legion of angels.

Armageddon . . . considered the site or time of the final battle between the physical phenomenon of good and the supernatural forces of evil foretold in Revelation 16:14-16 (KJV)

Athanasian Creed . . . a Christian document that originated in Europe about 400 A.D. which relates to the Trinity and incarnation.

B

baptism . . . a Christian act by which one is purified and sanctified by means of being immersed in water and cleansed spiritually.

beatitude . . . any of the declarations made in the Sermon on the Mount by Jesus.

Big Bang Theory . . . an astronomical hypothesis that deduces a cataclysmic birth of the universe from the observed expansion of the universe, cosmic radiation, an abundance of elements, and the laws of physics.

Bishop's Bible . . . an officially commissioned English translation of the Bible that was published in 1568 A.D.

blasphemous . . . the act of insulting, showing contempt or irreverence toward something considered sacred or inviolable.

Book of Mormon . . . the sacred book of the Church of Jesus Christ of Latter-Day Saints, believed by members of the church to be an abridgment by the prophet Mormon of a record of certain ancient peoples in America, written on golden plates, and discovered and translated (1827-30) by Joseph Smith.

Braham . . . the high god (or creator) of the Hindu triad.

C

communism . . . a system of social organization in which all economic and social activity is controlled by a totalitarian state dominated by a single and self-perpetuating political party.

confession . . . acknowledgment or disclosure of sin or sinfulness, especially to a priest to obtain absolution.

Copernican System . . . the belief that the earth rotates daily on its axis and the planets revolve in orbits around the sun.

creation . . . the act of bringing the world and all therein into ordered existence.

Creator . . . one of the names given to God.

crucify . . . a means of being put to death by nailing or binding wrists/hands and feet to a wooden cross.

Crusades . . . several military expeditions that took place from the 11th to 13th centuries (A.D.) to win the Holy Land from the Muslims. **cult** . . . a system of religious beliefs and rituals.

Czar . . . the name given to the ruler/emperor of Russia until the 1917 (A.D.) revolution.

D

deity . . . one exalted and revered as a supreme being, such as the ancient Greek/Roman gods and goddesses.

Depression . . . an economic condition characterized by substantial and protracted unemployment, low output and investment, etc; slump

divine . . . relating to or proceeding directly from the Creator (God).

dogma . . . a doctrine or series of doctrines concerning faith and/or morals formally stated and proclaimed by a church.

doctrine . . . a principle of writing (or a body of principles) in a branch of knowledge or a system of beliefs.

doomsday . . . considered a day of final judgment for mankind.

E

ecclesiastical . . . pertaining to the institution of a church and the clergymen.

edict . . . a decree issued by authoritative proclamation or command.

Emir . . . a chief, ruler or commander in Islamic countries.

empire . . . having a territory of great extent or a number of territories under imperial sovereignty rule.

empirical . . . based on observation or experience (such as data) without due regard for theory.

enigma . . . something that is hard to explain, define or understand; a mystery.

Enlightenment . . . a philosophic movement of the 18th century (A.D.) that was marked by the rejection of traditional social, religious and political ideas.

eschatology . . . a branch of theology concerned with the end of the world and the ultimate destiny of mankind.

Eucharist . . . a spiritual communion with God.

evil . . . something that is morally reprehensible, wicked or sinful.

evolution . . . historically known as a development of a biological group (such as race or species) having their origins in other preexisting types and that the distinguishable differences are due to modifications in successive generations.

extreme unction . . . a sacrament in which a priest anoints and prays for the recovery and/or salvation of an ill person.

F

faction . . . a religious group that is often contentious or self-seeking.

fornication . . . 1) excessive or blind adoration, reverence, devotion, etc. 2) voluntary sexual intercourse between two unmarried persons or two persons not married to each other.

freewill . . . the freedom of humans to make choices/decisions that are not determined by prior causes or by divine intervention.

G

Ghost Dance . . . a group dance of the late 19th century (A.D.) incorporated by an American Indian messianic sect believed to promote the return of the dead and restore the traditional ways of life.

God . . . the Supreme Being who is perfect in power, wisdom and goodness; who is worshiped as the creator and the ultimate ruler of the universe.

Great Spirit . . . the name given to the Creator by the American Native Indian.

H

Hebrew Bible . . . another name given to the holy scriptures of Judaism.

hegira . . . a journey or exodus undertaken to escape from a dangerous or undesirable situation.

Hellenism . . . a body of humanistic ideals associated with ancient Greece and including reason, the pursuit of knowledge, civic responsibility and bodily development.

holocaust . . . a thorough destruction involving extensive loss of life.

Holy Land . . . the land promised to the Jewish nation from the Creator (Yahweh).

hypothesis . . . a tentative assumption made in order to draw out and test its logical or empirical consequences.

I

idolatry . . . the worship, attachment or devotion of a physical object or symbol representing a god/gods.

immaculate conception . . . the conception of the virgin Mary, in which the dogma of the Roman Catholic Church decrees her soul was preserved free from original sin by divine grace.

incarnation . . . the union of divinity with humanity.

intermarriage . . . marriage between members of different groups, clans, race, creed, etc.

J

Jehovah . . . Jewish name given unto God (Creator)

jihad . . . any vigorous, emotional crusade for an idea or principle (usually associated with Islam's Holy wars)

K

Kabbalah . . . a medieval and modern thought system of Jewish philosophy, mysticism, and supernaturalism marked by belief in creation through origin and a code method of interpreting scripture in the Torah.

kingdom . . . a politically organized community or major territorial unit having a monarchical form of government headed by a king (or queen), emperor, pharaoh, etc.

Krishna . . . a deity of Hinduism worshiped as an incarnation of Vishnu.

L

Last Judgment . . . according to various theologies, this is the day of Allah's judgment of mankind during the 'End Times'.

Lotus Sutra . . . a central scripture of Mahayana Buddhism, emphasizing that anyone can attain enlightenment.

M

manna . . . a heavenly food miraculously supplied to the Hebrew nation during their journey through the wilderness during the days of Moses.

Messiah . . . the expected king and deliverer of the Jewish faith.

millennium . . . a period of 1000 years.

monarchy . . . a government having an hereditary ruler with life tenure and powers varying from nominal to absolute.

mosque . . . a religious building used for public worship by the Islamic nation.

N

natural selection . . . natural process that results in the survival and reproductive success of individuals/groups that leads to the perpetuation of genetic qualities best suited to that particular environment.

Nicene Creed . . . a Christian code of beliefs that expanded from the first Nicene council around 1596 (A.D.)

O

omnipresence . . . present in all places at all times.

original sin . . . the state of sin that according to Christian theology characterizes all of mankind as a result of Adam and Eve's fall from grace when they disobeyed [God].

origins . . . mankind's beginnings; ancestry and/or heritage.

P

papal . . . relating or pertaining to a pope or the Roman Catholic Church.

parable . . . a short story that illustrates a moral attitude or religious principle.

parchment . . . in antiquity, the skin of a sheep or goat for writing on.

Passover . . . a Jewish holiday beginning on the 14th of Nisan and commemorates the Hebrews liberation from slavery in Egypt.

penance . . . a sacramental rite that is practiced by Roman Catholic, Eastern (Greek) Orthodox and some Anglican churches and consists of private confession, absolution and atonement of sins.

Pharaoh . . . an ancient Roman king or emperor.

phenomena . . . an observable fact or event of scientific interest susceptible of scientific description and explanation.

polygamist . . . a person that has more than one spouse at the same time.

predestination . . . the belief that God (Creator), in consequence of his foreknowledge of all events, guides those who are destined for salvation.

Promised Land . . . commonly referred to as the place the Jewish nation inherits during the 'End Times'.

prophecy . . . a prediction of something to come as well as an inspired declaration of divine will and purpose.

Purgatory . . . according to Catholic doctrine: a place of punishment where the souls of those who died in God's good grace make amends for past sins and enter into heaven.

Q

quote . . . to speak or write (such as a passage) from another person; usually with credited acknowledgment.

R

rabbinical . . . relating or pertaining to the Jewish rabbi and/or their writings.

Reformation . . . a 16th century (A.D.) religious movement marked by the rejection or modification of some Roman Catholic doctrine and practice and established the Protestant churches.

reincarnation . . . a fresh embodiment and rebirth of a soul in a new body.

revelation . . . God's disclosure of his own nature and his purpose for mankind, especially through the words of human intermediaries.

S

sacrament . . . a Christian rite (such as baptism) that is believed to have been ordained by Jesus and that is held to by means of divine grace or to be a symbol of a spiritual reality.

Sanhedrin . . . the supreme council and tribunal of the Jews during post-exile times and headed by a High Priest and having religious, civil and criminal jurisdiction.

{Note: Sanhedrin was recently reinstated.}

Satan . . . the main adversary of the Creator (God) and Lord of evil in Judaism and Christianity.

schism . . . a formal division in or separation from a church or religious body.

scholar . . . a well learned person who has done advanced study in a special field.

sect . . . a religious group/denomination adhering to a distinctive doctrine or to a leader.

secular . . . not bound by monastic vows or rules and relating to certain clergy not belonging to a religious order or congregation.

seer . . . a person credited with extraordinary moral and spiritual insight.

Septuagint . . . a Greek version of the Jewish scriptures redacted in the 3rd and 2nd centuries (B.C.) by Jewish scholars and adopted by Greek-speaking Christians.

Setianism . . . a philosophy of the Temple of Set, founded in 1975 A.D., which adheres to enlightened individualism: enhancement and improvement of oneself by personal education, experiment and initiation.

Siva . . . the god of destruction and regeneration in the Hindu triad.

synagogue . . . the house of worship and communal center of a Jewish congregation.

Supreme Being . . . another name for God.

T

tabernacle . . . a place or house of worship for the Christians.

theocracy . . . a government, state or officials regarded as divinely guided.

theology . . . the study of religious faith, practice and experience and commonly made up of a distinctive body of theories and opinions.

transmigration . . . to go from one state of existence or place to another.

transmutation . . . the conversion of one element or nuclide into another either naturally or artificially.

tribunal . . . a type of court or forum of justice and something that decides and determines.

Tribulation Saints . . . a name given to the converts of Christianity after the Evangelical "Rapture" to face the Anti-Christ during the Great Tribulation.

Triumvirate . . . an office or government of triumvirs (a commission of three men)

U

Underworld . . . another name given to Hell; abode of the dead.

ungodly . . . denying or disobeying [God] or contrary to moral law.

Usher English Bible . . . biblical chronology published by Church of Ireland Archbishop James Usher (1581-1656) in which he purported to establish the time and date of the 'creation' as occuring in 4004 B.C. [according to the Julian calendar].

V

Vishnu . . . the preserver god of the sacred Hindu triad.

Vulgate . . . Latin Bible; authorized and used by the Roman Catholic Church.

W

Wycliffe Bible . . . the 1382 (A.D.) doctrine of John Wycliffe (c/1320-1384), in which he taught that all secular and ecclesiastical authority is derived from God and is forfeited by one who is in mortal sin, that the doctrine of transubstantiation is false and that monasticism is to be condemned.

X

==============

Y

Yahweh . . . the Hebrew (Jewish) name for God.

Z

Zoroastrianism . . . the religion and philosophy based on the teachings of Zoroaster, the prophet, and essentially synonymous with the worship of Ahura Mazda. Considered one of the oldest religions, it is uniquely important in history because of its possible formative links to both Western and Eastern religious traditions. Possibly had more influence on mankind directly or indirectly than any other faith.

About the Author

Kelly Warman-Stallings is a self-described literary multi-tasker. She is a local historian of the mid-Missouri area and has written and directed various public events, all while maintaining her wry wit, optimistic outlook, and most important of all her religious faith and deep sense of spirituality.

Born in Iberia, Missouri in 1960, Ms. Warman-Stallings grew up in Kansas City, Kansas which she still considers her hometown. She discovered the desire to write at the age of twelve through a simple, four-line poem. For many years poetry flowed from her pen. Poetry continues to be her first love in the literary genre.

Over the past twenty years she has written and published four books all dealing with local history and family genealogies. She credits her love of writing to her mother, who is a notable historian in her own right and a great inspiration to her daughter.

In addition to her writing, Ms. Warman-Stallings has directed plays and skits, and choreographed music talent shows. She was editor of a business-based newsletter in Jefferson City for six years. She is also a singer and song-writer.

Ms. Warman-Stallings currently lives in central Missouri. She has three children and six grandchildren.